A-Z of Ke... English

D0474850

A–Z of
Key Concepts in
Primary English

Elizabeth Randall and Averill Hardman

LearningMatters

For Joan, Rose and Marilyn

First published in 2002 by Learning Matters Ltd.

British Library Cataloguing in Publication Data
A CIP record for this book is available from the British Library.

ISBN 1 903300 47 9

Cover design by Topics — The Creative Partnership
Text design by Code 5 Design Associates Ltd
Project management by Deer Park Productions
Typeset by PDQ Typesetting
Printed and Bound in Great Britain by Bell & Bain Ltd, Glasgow

Learning Matters Ltd
58 Wonford Road
Exeter EX2 4LQ
01392 215560
info@learningmatters.co.uk
www.learningmatters.co.uk

Contents

Introduction

Teaching English in primary schools is a challenging and inspiring job. A key factor in effective teaching is subject knowledge. Good subject knowledge in English enables teachers to:

- plan and teach English well;
- prepare appropriate learning activities for children;
- challenge children in their learning;
- teach in a way that children understand;
- identify children's misconceptions and difficulties and intervene to ensure success;
- answer children's questions about English with confidence;
- impart knowledge about texts, sentences and words.

Working with trainee and new teachers highlighted the need for a handy reference guide to English teaching, one which embraced several aspects of English beneath one cover. This book aims to fulfil both these needs and provide quick access to definitions of English terms and concepts. Talk, as a tool for learning, and the consequent need to build a shared vocabulary to discuss English with children, plays a vital part in effective teaching. We hope this easy-to-use glossary of terms will help you to build this vocabulary successfully.

The *A–Z of Key Concepts in Primary English* has been written for:

- trainee and new teachers, as they continue to develop further their knowledge and understanding;
- experienced teachers, either supporting trainees in school placements or wishing to confirm their own subject knowledge;
- teaching assistants, supporting children in group and individual work.

The book is organised with straightforward alphabetical entries that are, when appropriate, cross-referenced to other items to help you make connections between key concepts. A margin icon like this and bold type has been used to highlight cross-references.

Also included are suggestions of other printed or electronic teaching resources that you might find useful in your planning and teaching. This icon appears when a resource is suggested.

Explicit links to National Literacy Strategy (NLS) publications are made throughout.

At the back of the book, you will find a list of useful resources including teaching resources, government publications, further reading to support your professional development, useful websites and high-quality software to use with your primary classes. We have also included at-a-glance lists of fiction and non-fiction text types (genres) and their features and the text types to be taught for each primary year group.

By its very nature, this book cannot (and does not) attempt to cover everything. It is designed to be used as part of a new teacher's toolkit, to confirm and develop understanding and to give confidence.

We hope you find this book informative and useful!

Elizabeth Randall and Averill Hardman
September 2002

A–Z of Key Concepts

abbreviation

A shortened form of a word or phrase, e.g. *cm/centimetre(s)*. Some common abbreviations are from Latin e.g. *ibid./ibidem meaning 'in the same place'*. Others are formed from the initial letters of the words which are pronounced individually, e.g. *YHA/Youth Hostels Association*. See **acronym**, **clipping** and **contraction**.

abstract noun

A type of noun referring to a feeling or intangible quality, e.g. *beauty, luck, happiness*. See diagram with **noun**.

accent

Difference in pronunciation often attributed to regional influences. British English has many different and recognisable accents, e.g. *Scouse and Cockney*. The accent which has had prestige in English is **received pronunciation (RP)** though this is no longer associated with one region.

acronym

An **abbreviation** created from the initial letters of a series of words which are pronounced as a word, e.g. *SMART targets (Specific, Measurable, Achievable, Relevant, Time-constrained)*.

acrostic

A type of poem where the initial letters of each line read from top to bottom make a word, e.g.

> *Soft*
> *Now falling*
> *On the ground*
> *White*

How to Teach Poetry Writing at Key Stage 1 and How to Teach Poetry Writing at Key Stage 2 (Morgan, 2001) are activity-based books of writing workshops linked to the NLS teaching objectives.

active voice

A construction where the subject of the verb (agent) carries out the action of the verb, e.g. *The birds ate the crumbs*. The passive form of this would be *The crumbs were eaten by the birds*. See **passive voice**.

adjective

A grammatical single word which gives information about a noun, modifies it and makes it specific, e.g. *a red bus, the spacious hall*. See **comparative**, **superlative** and **adjective phrase**.

3

adjective phrase

A group of words comprising an adjective and other words that function as a single adjective, e.g. *Her garden is <u>sunnier than mine</u>. The man <u>with dark hair</u> is my brother.*

adventure text

An entertaining text which allows escape from reality. It is structured chronologically with a series of action-packed events which provide excitement and tension for the reader, e.g. *Agent Z Stories by M. Haddon.* See **genre**.

Activities for Writing Adventure Stories (Powell, 2002) are ready-made photocopiable activities plus teacher's guide to help teachers to do shared and guided writing with the whole class and with groups.

adverb

A single word which often gives extra information about a verb, e.g. *She walked <u>slowly</u>.* The function of the adverb here is to specify the 'manner' of walking. Other adverb meanings include 'time', e.g. *Pete arrived <u>today</u>* and 'space' e.g. *Sue stepped <u>outside</u>.*

Adverbs can modify other words, e.g. *The new teacher spoke <u>very confidently</u>* (adverb + adverb). *She is <u>quite happy</u>.* (adverb + adjective). They can also modify whole sentences, e.g. *Really, you could do much better.*

adverbial

The inclusive term for the adverb element of clause structure that performs several functions:

- giving extra information about an event, e.g. *They crept <u>stealthily</u>;*
- linking clauses, e.g. *She met me as arranged. <u>However</u>, I was unable to stay very long;*
- commenting upon an event, e.g. *<u>Quite honestly</u>, I don't think that is the case.*

Adverbials may be **adverbial phrases** or single **adverbs**, and **adverbial clauses**. **Prepositional phrases** are often used as adverbials, e.g. *We played <u>in the park</u>.* Some **nouns** and **noun phrases** may also function as adverbials, e.g. *My friend phoned me <u>last night</u>.*

adverbial clause

A clause functioning as a single adverb, e.g. *We went for a walk in the park <u>before we went home</u>./We went for a walk in the park <u>later</u>.* The range of meanings conveyed by the adverbial element is very large; as well as time, manner and space, it includes reason, condition and result, e.g. *I ran <u>because I was late</u>* (answers question 'why'?). *You will see me <u>if I hurry</u>* (answers question 'on what condition'?). *I revised <u>so I passed the test</u>* (answers question 'with what result'?)

adverbial phrase

A group of words functioning as a single adverb, e.g. *We received the news very gladly.*

affective

Concerned with feelings and used in terms of a reader's response to a text. An affective question about a fiction text asks the reader to interpret motives, states of mind and emotions e.g. *In what ways did your feelings about the main character change throughout the book? How do you think King Midas felt when his daughter turned to gold?*

affix

A group of letters added to the beginning or end of a word. Letters added to the beginning make a prefix, e.g. *un*happy, *dis*please, *re*appear, *bi*lateral, and those added to the end make a **suffix**, e.g. joy*ful*, content*ment*, glad*ly*, inten*tion*.

agreement

A grammatical and visible link between parts of a sentence. There is agreement between subject and main verb e.g. *She goes/They go.* Parts of the sentence may agree in terms of **person, number, case** or **gender**. Another term for agreement is **concord.**

alliteration

The use of identical initial sounds in consecutive words to create a specific effect such as focusing attention upon the sound rather than the meaning of the words, e.g. *slippery, slithery snake; bees buzzing blindly.*

alphabet

In the English language, the system of representing sounds with 26 letters, 5 of them **vowels** and 21 **consonants**.

alphabetic code

A language system such as the one we have in English that works by representing sounds by letters or combinations of letters.

The National Literacy Strategy document, Progression in Phonics (DfEE, 2000, p.5), offers advice and information.

alphabetic method

A former method of teaching reading used from medieval to Victorian times in which children said the letter names in a word and then the whole word.

alphabetical order

The principle on which most reference books are organised ordering the items with those starting with A first right through to Z. Items beginning with the same letter are then ordered in alphabetical order of the second letter and so on.

ALS

Additional Literacy Support. This government initiative is being implemented with groups of junior school pupils to support and promote progress in literacy. It is additional to the normal English teaching they receive.

ambiguity

Lack of a single clear meaning. Words acquire new meanings and keep old ones at the same time, which may lead to **metaphor**. The potential for ambiguity may be exploited deliberately in **puns** or newspaper headlines, e.g. *'Railways on track at last!'*

analogy

Similarity between things which may provide a strategy for learning something new, e.g. *familiarity with spelling 'night' helping with 'fright'*, or provide a basis for **similes** and **metaphors**.

analytic phonics

an approach to teaching reading which involves using whole texts to help readers decode words in a meaningful context, making particular use of onset and rime. See **synthetic phonics**.

anecdote

An example based on personal experience given to enliven or illustrate a point.

annotation

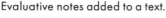

Evaluative notes added to a text.

In **miscue analysis** the text a child has read is **annotated** with symbols or notes to indicate the miscues or errors the child made in reading.

antonym

A word whose meaning is a near opposite of another, e.g. *dry/wet, truthful/ untruthful*.

aphorism

A short saying packed with meaning, e.g. *better safe than sorry; once bitten twice shy*.

apostrophe

1. A punctuation mark which shows possession, e.g. *the moon's surface, dogs' home/men's toiletries/the boss's car/the bosses' cars*.
2. A punctuation mark which shows letter omission, *we've/we have*.

appendix

A section at the end of a book or document providing additional information, such as research data.

article

A name for the **determiners** *a* and *an* (**indefinite**) and *the* (**definite**).

ascender

The part of a letter which rises above its main body, e.g. *h*, *d* and *b*.

aspect

This refers to the verb and how its action lasts over time. The action may be complete, ongoing or finished in the past but relevant to the present. Aspect has two facets: the perfective and the progressive.

The perfective uses the auxiliary 'have' in its present and past form and often conveys the idea of an action continuing up to a certain point in time. The progressive is made with 'be' and the 'ing' verb form and is used with the present and past tense and both perfective aspects. It conveys the idea of an event in progress. Another term for progressive is continuous.

Verb forms that are not progressive are termed simple. They convey the idea of a complete action.

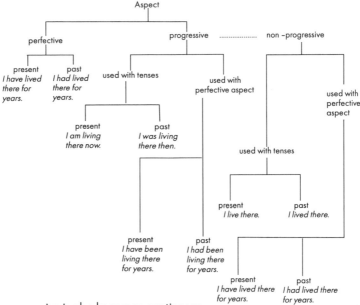

- progressive is also known as continuous
- non−progressive is also known as simple

assonance

The use of repeated vowel sounds in prose and poetry to create a specific effect such as focusing on the sound rather than the meaning of the words, e.g. *only the old oak groaned; calm, dark psalms in harmony.*

asterisk

A punctuation mark used to highlight an important word, one that is referred to in footnotes or as a replacement for an unacceptable word, e.g. ****!

audience

The intended listeners or readers who will influence the structural grammatical and **lexical** choices made by a writer when composing a text.

auditory

Related to hearing.

The auditory channel is important when teaching children to hear and identify sounds in words in the teaching of reading.

autobiography

A story written by someone about his or her own life and experiences which may be fact or fiction, e.g. *Fire, Bed and Bone by Henrietta Branford.*

auxiliary verb

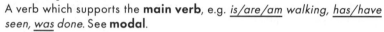

A verb which supports the **main verb**, e.g. *is/are/am* walking, *has/have* seen, *was* done. See **modal**.

ballad

A poem sometimes sung telling a story dramatically about a crucial event. The subjects of some old ballads are folk tales found in different versions all over Europe, while others commemorate popular heroes such as Robin Hood. Long lyrical ballads were written in the nineteenth century, e.g. *Coleridge's The Rime of the Ancient Mariner, Keats's La Belle Dame Sans Merci; Tennyson's The Lady of Shalott.*

base verb

The form of the verb as entered in a dictionary, which has no endings, e.g. *run, work.* It is sometimes called the **infinitive**.

bibliographic cue

A source of information comprising knowledge of books and how they work that can help readers decode and interpret texts.

bibliography

An appended list of titles and authors referred to in an essay or textbook.

big book

A large-format children's book which is frequently used by teachers in whole-class English teaching.

bilingual

Able to speak two languages.

biliterate

Able to write two languages.

binding

1. The process of fastening pages together into book form.
2. The paperback or hardback cover of a book.

biography

The story of a person's life written by another, e.g. *Anne Frank's Story by Carol Ann Lee; Leading Lives: J.F. Kennedy by David Downing; Famous People Famous Lives: William Shakespeare by Emma Fischel.*

bisyllabic

containing two syllables, e.g. *breakfast, basket, common.*

A useful way to help children identify syllables in spoken words is for them to hold their hand horizontally under the chin as they speak the word and count the number of times the chin touches the hand.

blank verse

Unrhymed verse with rhythm and metre usually written in lines of **iambic pentameter**, which is the normal line in Shakespeare's plays.

blend

1. To put separate sounds together to build up a word.
2. A blend is two consecutive consonant letters which are both pronounced and which occur frequently in words, e.g. initial blends: *sp, pl, cl, bl, fl, gl, sl, br, tr, cr, dr, fr, gr, pr.*

In **onset** and **rime** a blend can form the onset e.g. *play.*

The National Literacy Strategy document, Progression in Phonics (CfEE, 2000, p.4), offers advice and information.

blurb

A synopsis of a book provided on the back cover to interest and inform a prospective reader.

bold

Text in a darker print to make it stand out, e.g. *I am **not** prepared to help.*

book circle

A group of readers meeting regularly to discuss and review books read.

bottom-up

A processing strategy often referring to reading which uses what is on the page, namely letters and their matching sounds, and whole-word recognition to read the text. This contrasts with **top-down**.

boundary

In grammar the division between sentence parts or whole sentences which is usually marked by punctuation e.g. *word boundaries shown by spaces, sentence boundaries shown by full stops and capital letters.*

brackets

A pair of punctuation marks placed around words giving additional information in a sentence, e.g. *Sam and Sophie (their identical twins) were enjoying the birthday party.* Brackets may be called **parentheses.**

brainstorming

A technique for accessing prior ideas and generating new ones as a first stage in composition. It involves noting down appropriate words which may be used in the composition and may be a collaborative activity where all ideas are accepted. A **spidergram** or other visual/graphical form may be used to record the ideas.

browse

To look though a book or electronic text casually.

browser

Software that enables users to find their way round the Internet.

bullet point

A dot preceding an item in a list used as a presentational device to identify each item clearly. Sometimes the list is introduced by a colon at the end of the preceding text. Each bullet point starts a new line and the entry begins with a lower case letter. Formally each entry ends with a semi-colon apart from the final full stop.

calligram

A poem which is written in a form where layout, font and font size are an essential part of the meaning.

calligraphy

The art of handwriting. Illuminated lettering is an example of calligraphy and is a decorated initial letter or whole word, using gold, silver, colours and patterns and is often found in ancient manuscripts. In a classic text the first letter of each chapter is sometimes illuminated. The interwoven letters that create a personal monogram are also examples of calligraphy.

capital letter

The upper case form of a letter that is larger and sometimes a different shape from its lower case version, e.g. *ABC.*

caption

A title or heading accompanying an illustration, often found in non-fiction texts.

case

A set of endings added to nouns in some languages, e.g. *Latin*. In English only the **genitive** case is shown with nouns and it is made by adding 's' preceded by an **apostrophe** in writing e.g. *the girl's bike, the boss's car*. With the plural form of nouns which usually end in 's' the apostrophe is placed after the 's', e.g. *the girls' locker room*. In a few examples where the plural does not end in 's' an apostrophe followed by an 's' is used as in the singular, e.g. *the children's toys are on the floor*.

CD-Rom

Compact Disc Read Only Memory, a disc used in a computer or on a CD player.

chapter

A traditional division or coherent section of a fiction text, sometimes with a **heading**.

character

A created participant in a fiction text whose role is to further the plot and to engage the reader's interest on a human level as a personality. Characters may be humans, animals or (in science fiction) invented life forms.

characterisation

The way in which character is constructed by the writer. This may be by direct telling, *e.g. In Roald Dahl's 'Fantastic Mr. Fox' we learn about the three farmers: Boggis, Bunce and Bean. 'They were rich men. They were also nasty men. All three of them were about as nasty and mean as any men you could meet.'*

Characters may also be constructed more indirectly through their actions. In *'Skellig'* by David Almond, Mina spends a great deal of time on her own observing and drawing birds and protecting them from danger. The reader may infer certain things about her nature from this.

Other indirect ways of creating character include the use of speech. Philip Ridley uses dialogue, in particular the individual catchphrases used by characters, to suggest character traits, e.g. *King Streetwise in 'Kaspar and the Glitter' addresses everyone as 'my moonlit dudes'. Hushabye Brightwing, his ex-girlfriend, refers to others as 'Brother' or 'Sister'.*

Besides these devices, **setting** may play a part in character creation, e.g. *In 'Owl Babies' by Martin Waddell the scary setting makes the little owl seem very brave.*

Physical appearance may also provide strong clues as to character, e.g. *In 'Where the Wild Things Are' by Maurice Sendak Max takes on some physical features of the monsters.*

chart
A visual representation of information in table form.

checklist
1. A list of criteria against which achievement may be measured, e.g. *a checklist of reading behaviours linked to the skills and knowledge children need to become fluent readers.*
2. A memory aid which could help children to organise their writing.

choral speech
Speaking in unison that may be part of dramatic performance.

chronological
In time order, which is an underlying principle for many genres, e.g. *diaries, recounts, instructions.* See entry **non-chronological.**

cinquain
A poem with five lines and 22 syllables organised as a sequence of 2, 4, 6, 8, 2 as in

> *hedgehog*
> *your brush of spikes*
> *protects you from most harm*
> *but not the gaping cattle grid*
> *alas!*

classic
A text with wide readership that has gained status over time and is considered a standard of its genre, e.g. *The Hobbit by J.R.R. Tolkien, The Secret Garden by Frances Hodgson Burnett.*

clause
A unit below the sentence in the hierarchy of grammar. A clause is a set of words containing a verb. A sentence with one clause that can stand alone is a simple sentence, e.g. *I read a book.* Sentences made from more than one clause may be **compound** or **complex.**

clerihew
A humorous poem of two rhyming couplets with the first of its four lines being a person's name, e.g.

> *Cinderella*
> *got a fella.*
> *Ugly sisters*
> *just got blisters.*

cliché
An expression that has lost originality through overuse, e.g. *as good as gold.*

climax

The culmination of events in a story creating the point of highest tension for the reader.

clipping

Shortening of words of two or more syllables, e.g. *exam/examination, fridge/refrigerator.*

cloze

A procedure whereby certain words in a text are omitted for readers to provide alternatives that make sense. The omissions may be selected on different criteria, e.g. *word class.* Cloze is used to promote comprehension and can foster oral language skills if carried out as a collaborative activity. It may also be used to investigate a particular writer's style.

cluster

A consonant cluster is a group of consonants often occurring together in words, e.g. *spr, spl.*

coherence

The overall logic of a text and the sense that an audience can make of it through inferential reading or listening.

cohesion

The sense made by a text through explicit links created within and between sentences, often through pronouns and connectives, e.g. *A bottle had been washed up on the beach. There it lay beneath some seaweed. As a result the bottle and its contents were not discovered for some time.*

collage

A composition made up of different images or textures put together and often used in picture books, e.g. *Window by Jeannie Baker.*

collective noun

A type of noun referring to single individuals as a group, as in *committee, team, school.* The plural verb form is often used, e.g. *The away team were losing at half time.*

collocation

A combination of words often found together, e.g. *poached, boiled* and *eggs.* Collocation helps readers to predict words. Unexpected collocations may be used to create vivid images by poets and pop groups looking for a memorable name, e.g. *The Grateful Dead, The Electric Soft Parade.*

colloquial

Informal conversational language which may contain non-standard forms, e.g. *ain't, OK, right?*

colon
A punctuation mark that may introduce a list, what is said or an example. It may be used between clauses to mark the separation between them, e.g. *The night was dark: the house was illuminated by clusters of candles of every shape and size.*

comma
A punctuation device that marks grammatical boundaries, e.g. *She ordered pizza, French fries, salad and juice.* The commas separate individual words and phrases in this list, but they can also mark off clauses within sentences, e.g. *Because it was dark, we wore reflective clothing.*

commentary
Additional notes or explanatory material to further understanding of a text.

common noun

One of the main categories of noun. Common nouns are names of things, e.g. *nephew, sky, table, paper.* They usually have a plural as well as singular form e.g. *nephew/nephews.* They may be preceded by a **determiner**, e.g. *my nephew, the sky.* See **noun**.

communication
The act of giving and receiving messages in speech, listening, writing, reading and other non verbal forms.

comparative adjective
The form of an adjective used when comparing one item with another, e.g. *bigger than.* To make the comparative the suffix 'er' is added to the adjective or the word 'more' is used with it e.g. *nervous/more nervous.* Irregular forms include *good/better* and *bad/worse.* See **superlative.**

complement
An element in the clause that gives more information about the subject or object, e.g. *Ben is a very thoughtful person.* As well as the verb 'to be', other verbs can link the subject and complement, e.g. *seem, feel.*

complex sentence
A sentence with more than one **clause**, one or more of which is a **subordinate clause**, e.g. *After she had finished supper, she went to bed. When she was tired she switched off the light so that she could go to sleep.*

complication
The problem which initiates the plot of a story.

compose
To put together a piece of writing, constructing it according to the accepted structure of a particular text type. See **genre**.

composite text

A text whose meaning derives from both words and illustrations together.

composition

A completed piece of work that has been created by an individual or group. In writing composition includes both planning (which means thinking about content, audience and purpose) and composing (selecting appropriate vocabulary and sentence structure).

compositional skills

The lexical, grammatical and organisational skills that are involved in putting together a written text. These skills are detailed in the National Curriculum programme of study for writing, and in the text and sentence level strands of the National Literacy Strategy.

compound sentence

A sentence with two clauses of equal weight joined by a **coordinating conjunction**, e.g. *They went to the disco and they enjoyed themselves.*

compound word

A new word made up of two or more words which could each stand alone. Different word classes may enter into these combinations as in noun + noun, e.g. *handbag*, adjective + noun e.g. *gentleman*, verb + grammatical word, e.g. *go–between*. Hyphens are found in some compound words, as in the last example.

comprehension

The process of understanding the meaning of a text. See **semantic** and **DARTS**. Teachers' use of different kinds of questions can promote children's understanding of texts. Comprehension is taught in **text level** work in the literacy hour.

Literacy Land *published by Longman includes a reading programme (Story Street), large-format books, photocopiable writing resources, comprehension activities and teachers' notes to support teaching in the literacy hour.*

conclusion

The final section of a text which draws it to an end.

concord

Sometimes called **agreement**, this refers to the link between subject and verb, e.g. *He was frightened and they were frightened.* Nouns as **complements** show number concord, e.g. *That is a joke.*

C

concrete noun

A type of noun that can be seen and measured, e.g. *book, thermometer, bicycle, island*. See diagram under **noun.**

concrete poem

A poetic form whose shape and visual appearance reflect the subject matter.

conference

A dialogue or interview conducted between teacher and pupil as a form of assessment, e.g. *a literacy conference*, yielding information about attitude to reading (or writing), preferences, subject matter or knowledge of reading strategies.

conjunction

A word class whose function is to link clauses in a sentence. **Coordinating conjunctions** e.g. *and, but, so*, may link clauses of equal status creating a **compound** sentence. **Subordinating conjunctions**, e.g. *although, because, when, that*, introduce **subordinate clauses** within a **complex** sentence.

connective

A word or phrase which connects or links clauses or sentences in order to provide **cohesion**, e.g. *Everyone is in agreement. <u>As a result</u>, we will return to work on Monday.*

Connectives may be conjunctions or adverbials:

- conjunctions join clauses within a sentence, *e.g. I was sad but I concealed it;*
- adverbials join sentences and link them, *e.g. I was sad. However, I concealed it.*

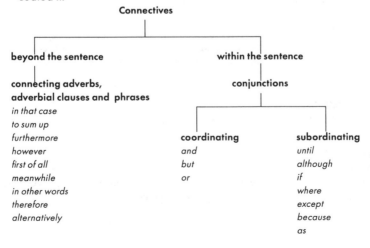

Connectives	
beyond the sentence	**within the sentence**
connecting adverbs, adverbial clauses and phrases	**conjunctions**
in that case	
to sum up	

coordinating	**subordinating**
furthermore	
however	*and*	*until*
first of all	*but*	*although*
meanwhile	*or*	*if*
in other words		*where*
therefore		*except*
alternatively		*because*
		as

conscience alley

A **drama strategy** which supports decision-making through listening to opposing advice from two groups of people in lines facing each other before a final choice is made.

consonant

All the letters in the alphabet apart from a, e, i, o, u.

consonant digraph

Two consonant letters (graphs), e.g. *ck, th, ch, ll, sh, pn, kn, ng*, representing one sound (phoneme).

consonant phoneme

The sounds made by the consonants in the alphabet.

Consonant phonemes	Examples words showing representations of the different phonemes
/b/	**b**all, ro**bb**er
/c/	**c**ome, **k**ettle, **ch**aos, ba**ck**, **q**uiet, bo**x**
/d/	**d**anger, ri**dd**le, shou**ld**
/f/	**f**all, sta**ff**, **ph**oto, enou**gh**
/g/	**g**irl, da**gg**er
/h/	**h**en
/j/	**j**ingle, lar**ge**, do**dge**, **g**esture
/l/	**l**ittle, do**ll**
/m/	**m**ine, gli**mm**er, du**mb**
/n/	**n**ever, bo**nn**et, **gn**ome, **pn**eumatic, **kn**ee
/p/	**p**art, wra**pp**er
/r/	**r**at, bo**rr**ow, **wr**ite
/s/	**s**it, mi**ss**ing, **c**eiling, **sc**ene, hou**s**e, fen**ce**
/t/	**t**ent, ma**tt**er
/v/	**v**est, groo**ve**
/w/	**w**all
/y/	**y**ellow
/z/	**z**ero, wa**s**, new**s**, ro**se**
/ch/	**ch**in, ca**tch**
/ng/	wro**ng**, li**nk**
/sh/	**sh**ell, pre**ss**ure, **ch**ef, cau**ti**on
/th/	**th**umb
/th/	**th**is
/zh/	mea**s**ure

The National Literacy Strategy document, Progression in Phonics (DfEE, 2000, pp. 5 and 6), offers advice and information.

17

content word

A word which carries meaning and is thus included when notes are made. Whereas the number of grammatical words in the English language remains constant, the number of content words is constantly growing. See **loan words** and **lexis**.

contents page

A page at the beginning of a book which sets out what is contained in the book and gives the page numbers relating to specific information.

contextual cue

Helpful support from the surrounding text which readers draw on when decoding the meaning of a specific word or sentence.

continuous text

Text in full sentences, not in note form or **bullet points**.

contraction

A shortened form, usually of a verb, where omitted letters are marked by an apostrophe, e.g. *they've, can't, I'm.* One apostrophe replaces one or more omitted letters.

coordination

The process of linking two clauses of equal status with a coordinating **conjunction**.

correspondence

The matching of letters with their phonemes or a spoken word with a written one. In learning to read, young children are taught letter/sound correspondences.

count noun

A type of noun which with its singular and plural forms can refer to a single item or many, e.g. *chair/chairs.* See **noun** and **mass noun**.

couplet

Two consecutive lines of verse which rhyme with each other, e.g.

Icy wind that stings and blows
freezing forehead, chilling nose.

cover

The outside of a book, either hardback or paperback, usually having an illustration, title and names of author/s and illustrator, that aims to inform and attract the reader.

creative writing

Part of English lessons in the 1960s, this meant imaginative composition that could involve individual writing in response to a sensory stimulus such as music or a first-hand experience. The writer was encouraged to respond using all of the senses and the personal, compositional aspect of the process was paramount.

critique
To analyse and critically review a text or discussion.

cue
A source of information often used in the context of reading, e.g. phonic cue, *graphic cue, visual cue, semantic cue, syntactic cue, bibliographic cue.* Some of these are called 'searchlights' in the National Literacy Strategy.

cursive
Written with letters joined together by **ligatures** in a flowing style. Children need to use joined writing in order to achieve level three in the National Curriculum attainment targets. Entry and exit strokes on each letter are sometimes taught at the initial stages before the achievement of a full cursive hand.

The National Literacy Strategy document, Developing Early Writing (DfEE, 2001, p.162), offers advice and information.

cut and paste
A technique used when revising and editing work on the computer when the writer wants to move text around or delete parts of it. Cutting is the removal of a section of text. Pasting is the replacement of that section elsewhere.

CVC
A letter string comprising consonant, vowel and consonant, e.g. *sit.* The word 'twist' would be represented as CCVCC. Many other vowel and consonant combinations are possible.

DARTS
Directed Activities Related to Texts — procedures to develop comprehension skills. Activities include **sequencing, cloze, grouping, labelling, modelling.**

dash
A punctuation mark which may be used in pairs instead of brackets or may replace other punctuation marks in notes or informal letters, e.g. *She walked boldly — albeit reluctantly — to confess her crime.*

debate
Discussion between parties who offer views for and against an issue.

declarative

The structure of **statements** which is subject followed by verb, e g. *They left at midnight*. See **interrogative, exclamative, imperative**.

deconstruction

Identification of the structural components of a text so that they may be analysed.

deduction

The process of reasoning or drawing out information from a text which is not stated literally. The National Curriculum Key Stage 2 English programme of study states that pupils should be taught to use deduction and **inference** in their reading of texts.

demonstration

1. A whole-class teaching technique used to initiate shared writing whereby the teacher models composing strategies and writes (**scribes**) examples for the pupils.
2. A whole-class teaching technique where the teacher models reading strategies.

   The process is described in detail in the National Literacy Strategy publications *Grammar for Writing* (DfEE, 1999, p.15) *Developing Early Writing* (DfEE, 2002), and *Progression in Phonics* (p. 10).

denouement

The outcome when the problem which has arisen in a story is untangled and the issues resolved.

derivation

The tracing of a word back to its source.

derivational morpheme

A type of affix that is added to the beginning or end of a word. This makes a difference in either word class, as in the change from noun to adjective e.g. *truth/truthful*, or in the meaning e.g. *organise/disorganise*.

descender

The part of a letter which extends below the main body of the letter, e.g. *y, p*.

descriptive language

Language which aims to create a mood, paint a vivid scene or to be informative about the subject in the text or talk. **Adjectives, adverbs and verbs** may feature prominently.

determiner

A word class used in certain positions before nouns to make the nouns specific. They include the articles *a, an, the* and numbers, e.g. *the three dogs*. Examples of other determiners include *all, several, much, this, that*.

developmental checklist

A list of criteria relating to reading or writing behaviours that is organised from simplest to most complex and against which individual attainment may be informally assessed.

Dewey decimal

A system by which library books in this country are usually classified.

diachronic variation

The way language changes over a period of time.

diacritic

A mark or point attached to letters to show differences in sound. In German, for instance, the vowels a, o and u change their sounds when two dots (the umlaut) are placed above them.

diagram

Pictorial representation of information often found in non-fiction texts.

dialect

A variety of oral language which incorporates both accent (pronunciation) and the use of regional words and different grammar. Dialects may also be written and used in dialogue in fiction to create characterisation, e.g. *Burglar Bill by Janet and Allan Ahlberg, A Walk in the Park by Anthony Browne, A Tea-Leaf on the Roof by Jean Ure.*

dialectal variation

The way that language varies because of regional or social differences between speakers.

dialogue

Conversation between two or more people.

diary

A book or text in which the writer notes his or her day-to-day experiences and may comment on these, e.g. *Zlata's Diary by Zlata Filipovic.* A diary may be written by an imagined author based on historical evidence gathered by a modern writer in order to entertain as well as educate, e.g. *The Lost Diary of Julius Caesar's Slave by Steve Barlow and Steve Skidmore.*

diatypic variation

The way that language changes according to purpose and intended audience.

diction

Word choice, pronunciation and articulation in speech.

dictionary
a reference book which lists words alphabetically and gives their meaning.

diglossia
A situation where two varieties of a language exist, one a standard and the other of lower status, that are used for different purposes in the same community. In South Asia there are languages that have higher literary forms which are very different from the spoken versions, e.g. *Hindi, Urdu.*

digraph
Two letters representing one **phoneme**, e.g. /sh/, /ch/.

diminutive
1. A word formed from another meaning a smaller version of the type sometimes suggesting affection, e.g. *notelet, novelette, lambkin.*
2. A word used with the adjectives 'little' or 'tiny', e.g. *Little Women, Tiny Tears.*

direct speech
Words that are spoken and signalled by the use of speech marks, e.g. 'Hello, John. It's good to see you.'

directionality
The principle by which English letters and words are written and read from left to right and from top to bottom on the page. It also refers to the starting point and subsequent clockwise/anti-clockwise movement in the formation of letters in handwriting.

directives
Often called commands, these sentences pass on good wishes and request, invite or warn someone to do something, e.g. *Please lower your heads on this deck! Enjoy your meal! Best of luck!*

directory
A book containing the names and addresses of residents of a place, e.g. *telephone directory.*

discourse
1. Spech, spoken language.
2. Context-specific spoken language practices or a speech genres, *e.g. the type of spoken language teachers use only in the school setting.*

discrimination
The ability to differentiate and distinguish between items such as sounds or letter shapes.

discussion text
Presents the different viewpoints in an argument and comes to a conclusion.

double negative

Use of two **negatives** (now considered a non-standard or dialectal form), e.g. *I never saw nobody.* The standard form would be *I never saw anybody.*

doublespread

1. The two pages of a picture book that face each other.
2. An article spread across two pages which face each other.

doubling

Use of the same letter consecutively, e.g. *skipped.*

A useful rule in spelling is that in verbs ending in a single vowel plus a consonant, the final consonant is doubled before adding a suffix, e.g. *hop – hopped; run – running.*

When a single syllable verb ends with a double vowel plus a consonant, the final consonant is not doubled, e.g. *read/reading; spread/spreading.*

In the case of verbs with more than one syllable ending in a <u>stressed</u> vowel followed by a consonant, the final consonant is doubled before adding a suffix, *e.g. refer/referred; propel/propelled.*

In the case of verbs with more than one syllable, ending in an <u>unstressed</u> vowel followed by a consonant, the final consonant is not doubled before adding a suffix, *e.g differ/differing; bracket/bracketed.*

download

To move an item from the Internet to a personal computer.

draft

A version of a text produced before a final copy.

In producing a written text, pupils may produce several drafts, **revising** and **editing** until the final version is achieved.

drama

A physical acting out of an oral or textual composition (play) with others and sometimes before an audience.

The NATE (2001) publication Cracking Drama: Progression in Drama within English is a valuable resource for teaching drama at Key Stages 1 and 2.

drama strategy

A technique within drama for exploring an issue, character or text, e.g. **thought-tracking; mantle of the expert; hot-seating; role play; conscience alley; forum theatre.**

The NATE publications by Grainger and Cremin Resourcing Classroom Drama 5-8 (2001) and Resourcing Classroom Drama 8–14 (2001) provide useful teaching strategies.

dry-wipe board

1. A large surface for teachers to write on, which the class can all see. This is a resource which is used in demonstrating and modelling in the teaching of writing.

2. A small surface for pupils to write on, show to the teacher and clean for reuse. It may be used in shared and guided writing, and supported composition.

dual language book

A book printed in two languages.

dyslexia

A specific language difficulty which may involve difficulties in some aspects of reading and writing.

EAL

English as an Additional Language. Recommendations for teaching children for whom English is an additional language are included in the introduction to the National Curriculum. There is information about how best to support these pupils in English lessons in the National Literacy Strategy Framework for Teaching.

Early Literacy Support.

ELS is additional support for reading and writing that is given to selected pupils for 20 minutes each day in Year 1, term 2 in primary schools for 12 weeks. The groups are often taught by trained learning support assistants.

edit

To amend a written **draft** before publication, checking for factual accuracy and improving aspects of style, grammar or spelling.

The National Literary Strategy document, Grammar for Writing *(DfEEE, 1999, p.190), offers advice and information.*

editorial

A text written by an editor or lead writer in a newspaper or journal which may explore and express an opinion on a current issue and outline other articles contained in the publication.

elegy

A poem of mourning or a funeral song, e.g. *Elegy Written in a Country Churchyard by Thomas Gray; Elegy on the Death of a Mad Dog by Oliver Goldsmith.*

ellipsis

1. An ellipsis is the three dots representing a pause in a text and implying something understood to be filled in.
2. The omission of words whose inclusion would be a repetition of what has already been said and understood, e.g. *He wanted to catch the last train, but couldn't.*

embedded

Dependent upon a main clause and thus a **subordinate clause**. It can also mean 'contextualised' when referring to early reading behaviour.

emergent

Denoting a reader or writer whose skills are just beginning to develop.

Emergent writing refers to a developmental approach to the teaching of writing which relies on pupils learning through making independent attempts, at their own level, without the intervention of the teacher, drawing on any knowledge they may have to write the text. It allows the pupil to concentrate on composition without worrying about correct spelling and properly formed handwriting. Children's very early writing is referred to as 'mark making with intent' in the National Literacy Strategy document *Developing Early Writing* (DfEE, 2002, p. 166).

empathy

An **affective** response whereby one person acknowledges how another is feeling and understands his or her point of view. It is used when discussing a reader's response to a character in a text, e.g. *How do you think one of the characters would explain his/her actions in the final chapters of the book? How do you think the little owl feels? Why do you think he feels like that?*

enactment

The conversion of a text from written to dramatic form by acting out the text or a scene from it.

encode

To spell and write using phonic skills, analogy and prior knowledge to build up the text.

encyclopaedia

A **reference** text often illustrated and organised in alphabetical order, which contains general knowledge information.

endpapers

The first and final pages of a book that are stuck down to the covers.

entry stroke

A short line leading into a letter which is practised, in some handwriting styles, as a preparatory stage before **cursive** script.

envoy

A role in discussion work as a messenger sent from one group to another to report and share ideas or information.

epic

1. A long poem in narrative form relating the heroic deeds of a legendary character, e.g. *The Pied Piper of Hamelin by Robert Browning.*

2. An epic may also be a long story or long running serialised novel on television.

eponym

A person who gives his or her name to something, e.g. *Napier's Bones, Cuisenaire rods, to do a Delia.*

ERIC

Everyone Reading In Class — a time set aside for all the class to undertake silent reading.

etymology

The study of the original meanings of words, their derivation and history.

eulogy

A written or spoken text praising something or someone, often a person who has recently died.

evaluation

A considered judgement about the merits and demerits of a piece of work. An evaluative question about a text asks the reader to give an opinion, which is an advanced skill, e.g. *Have you learned anything about human beings and how they should treat each other from this book? Why do you think the author chose to use dialect for the speech of the main character?* See National Curriculum Key Stage 2.

events

What happens in a story, recount or report. In these genres events are usually arranged chronologically. See **speech event** and **literacy event**.

exclamative

The sentence structure of speech that expresses an emotion. Exclamations can be **minor** sentences, e.g. *Goodness me!* They can also have the structure of **major** sentences with 'what' or 'how' followed by subject then verb, e.g. *How kind you are!*

exclamation mark
A punctuation mark that signals an exclamation, *e.g. What a surprise!*

exit stroke
A short line leading away from a letter which is found in some handwriting styles as a preparatory stage before **cursive** writing.

explanation
A text type whose purpose is to explain how something works or give reasons for a natural or social phenomenon. The structure includes an introductory description of the topic followed by a step–by–step account of how or why something happens. Time connectives such as 'next' and causal connectives such as 'therefore' feature in such texts. Verbs are usually in the present simple tense and may be in the passive voice, e.g. *Kites are kept in the air by differences in air pressure on their upper and lower surfaces.*

expressive reading
Reading aloud that conveys meaning and feeling vividly and is appropriate to the grammar of the text. This skill is a sentence level objective in the National Literacy Strategy from from Y1.

extended writing
Writing undertaken for a period of time which may produce a whole, complete text. Schools often plan a special time for this beyond the literacy hour.

fable
A moral tale in prose or poetry that sometimes uses animals to reveal human weaknesses. Jean de la Fontaine and Aesop are renowned fable writers of the past. Tony Ross and Vivian French have produced contemporary versions of some of their tales.

fact
Something that is true and is known to have happened. See **non-fiction**.

fairy tale
A children's story with archetypal characters, often set in the past and using recognisable devices such as challenges, magic numbers and patterns of language. Themes may include conflict between good and evil, e.g. *Beauty and the Beast, Sleeping Beauty.*

Activities for Writing Fairy Stories (Braund and Gibbon, 2001) is a collection of ready-made photocopiable activities plus teacher guidance that helps teachers to do shared and guided writing with the whole class or with groups.

fantasy

A fiction genre that aims to entertain and provide an exciting escape from reality. Its main ingredients are an imaginative plot, unusual characters and an element of magic. Writers of fantasy include Terry Pratchett, Susan Cooper, Lynne Reid Banks, Helen Cresswell and Kaye Umansky.

Activities for Writing Fantasy Stories (Lovatt, 2001) is a collection of ready-made photocopiable activities plus teacher guidance that helps teachers to do shared and guided writing with the whole class or with groups.

fiction

Writing which is not representing the truth, e.g. *stories*. Fiction genres include science fiction, adventure stories, myths, legends, traditional stories.

Read and Respond from Scholastic is a set of books with photocopiable activities based on a selection of fiction texts by well known children's authors. The activities focus children on comprehension and features of genre, character, plot, setting, grammar, punctuation, dialogue, vocabulary and spelling.

Literacy Line-up from Evans Education consists of fiction and non-fiction books for Key Stage 2 and includes teachers' books

figurative language

Language comprising **metaphors** and **similes** which are used to create particular moods in texts.

final

The last letter of a word occupies a final position.

finite verb

A verb form that has contrasts of **tense**, **number**, **person** and **mood** and a subject with which it agrees.

flashcard

A card with a word written on it used for teaching children to read by visual recognition of the whole word. Sets of these are sometimes included in published reading schemes or packages.

flowchart

A diagram clearly showing a sequence to be followed, such as the steps to be taken when making something, often using direction arrows to mark the order.

flyer

A sheet of paper printed with a message or information. The National Literacy Strategy has produced useful flyers to support teachers in their literacy teaching.

flyleaves

The blank first and last leaves of a completed book.

folk tale

An oral or written story which is passed down through generations within and across cultures, e.g. *Tortoise's Dream*, which is an African folk tale, told by J. Troughton. *Russian Folk Tales* by James Riorden. See **genre**.

font

A style of printed text. Fonts have individual names, e.g. *Sassoon Primary, Comic Sans, Times New Roman.*

foot

A unit of stress or rhythm that consists of one or more syllables. Many stress patterns are possible. An iambic foot, for example, comprises an unstressed and stressed syllable. Shakespeare often used five iambic feet per line in his blank verse, e.g. Oberon's speech in Midsummer Night's Dream, II.ii:

And with / the juice / of this / I'll stain / her eyes,
And make / her full / of hate / ful fan / tasies.

footnote

Additional information given at the bottom of a page rather than in the main text.

form

The visual appearance of a word or text.

formal

A **register** of language used in official or public contexts that contrasts with casual, informal usage.

format

Book size and shape. See **landscape** and **portrait**.

forum theatre

A **drama strategy** whereby a scene is created jointly by both actors and audience drafting and redrafting ideas to explore meaning or represent a text as accurately as possible.

frame

The boundary between a picture and the page shown as a white margin or a decorated border; one small section of a comic strip, illustrated story or film. Manipulating the frame provides the illustrator with many ways of creating meaning in texts. Framing can affect the pace and order of reading, can draw readers in or distance them from the action, and can create tension when the frame is broken.

free verse
Poetry without regular patterns in terms of rhyme and rhythm.

freeze frame
A **drama strategy** whereby a moment in time is captured by a still image created by people working in role.

front
To give prominence to part of a sentence by moving it to the beginning, e.g. *High in the sky they flew.*

frontispiece
An illustration in the front of a book before the text.

FTP
File Transfer Protocol — the language used for moving files round the Internet.

full stop
A punctuation mark that shows a sentence boundary.

function
The role a language item performs.

functional grammar
A model of grammar which states that language structures are related to the purpose to which language is put and which recognises that change is inherent in such a system. In a functional grammar words have names, *e.g. noun,* and other descriptors which refer to their role in a sentence, *e.g. subject.*

functional language
Oral language which has a practical, utilitarian use.

future 'tense'
The type of verb used to refer to events in the future. In English this is not a true tense because it does not have a separate form with its own endings. It uses the present tense form, *e.g. He leaves on Monday; He is leaving on Monday,* or the base infinitive with an auxiliary, *e.g. He will leave on Monday.*

gender
Grammatical gender is the way in which some languages, though not English, group nouns by the type of ending they have or by words accompanying them in the noun phrase, e.g. *la casa* (f.) *means 'the house' in Spanish and el libro (m) means 'the book'.* In English, a contrast of female and male gender is restricted to pronouns, e.g. *he/she, him/her, his/hers and himself/herself.*

generic structure
The composition of texts that share common elements because they share a

similar purpose. The text type and its features are recognisable and can be used as models for writing in the same **genre.**

genitive

A **case** whose main meaning is 'possession', e.g. *my daughter's room = her room.*

genre

A type of text with identifiable structure and language features, *e.g. instructional genre, recount.* See the tables of features of fiction and non-fiction texts at the end of the book.

Oxford Literacy web Launch into Literacy from Oxford University Press includes a range of materials including posters, flipover teacher demonstration books, big books, children's books in a range of fiction and non-fiction genres, and teachers' books.

genre exchange

The process of changing one text type into another, such as writing a story in the form of a poem. This highlights the linguistic features of the different genres for pupils.

gerund

A former term for the **participle** ending in 'ing'. This participle functions as a noun, *e.g. Swimming is my favourite hobby; The gathering of the clans.*

gesture

A non-verbal means of communication, e.g. *shrugging shoulders, wagging the index finger.* Some gestures may be culture specific e.g. *'Thumbs up' is a sign of agreement in British culture but may be interpreted differently in other cultures.*

glossary

An alphabetically ordered list placed at the back of a book defining specific terms used and highlighted in the text.

grammar

An analysis of a language based on the study of how sentences are constructed and how they work. Grammar is sometimes referred to as **syntax.**

The National Literacy Strategy Grammar for Writing document and the Grammar Show CD Rom from Sherston Software will be useful to help you plan and teach grammar. The video Grammar from the BBC and Big Book Grammar by Palmer and Morgan (200) which includes differentiated activities for group/independent work are also helpful resources.

grapheme

A letter of the alphabet written down or printed. Some phonemes have several different graphemic forms, e.g. *the phoneme /ay/ may be written as 'ai', 'ay', 'a-e'.*

graphic
Relating to what is written down.

graphology
The written medium of language and all the resources needed by the system to communicate in this form.

grapho-phonic cue
The phonetic and graphic knowledge that can be used as a source of information to help a reader decode a text.

grid
A matrix on which to record researched information in the form of notes which can be used as a basis for writing.

ground
The area of a picture into and against which people and objects are placed, which may be separated into background, middle ground and foreground. This may be alluded to when teachers are discussing the front cover and illustrations in a big book in whole-class shared reading, guided or individual reading. The positioning may highlight setting and characters in a story.

grouping
A **DARTS** comprehension activity involving sectioning parts of a text that fit one category, such as listing all the adjectives describing an object or character.

guided reading
The part of the literacy hour devoted to the teacher working with an attainment group on specific reading objectives related to reading strategies, comprehension, features of texts and responding to texts.

guided writing
Essentially a mini writing lesson that can be a step towards independent writing. It currently takes place in the context of the literacy hour. The teacher works with a specific attainment group for 20 minutes on a task that will provide appropriate challenge. The purpose of guided writing is to give support with planning, drafting, revising, editing or evaluating work following on from what has been taught in shared writing sessions. Generally the class is divided into five attainment groups. Each group has a guided reading or writing session with the teacher once a week.

half rhyme
Words which nearly rhyme, *e.g. peace and pace; silent and salient.*

haiku
A poetic form comprising three lines of 5, 7 and 5 syllables. Haiku create a brief visual image, often of the natural world, e.g.

daffodils alert
pertly poised on slender stalks
sentinels of Spring.

hand-gym

A collection of everyday objects used to give young children practice in the fine motor skills that will be needed in handwriting, such as pinching or twisting movements.

handwriting

The skill of physically putting communicative marks on paper. Print and cursive scripts are taught in primary schools. There are different styles of handwriting taught, e.g. *Kingston.*

head

The noun or verb in a phrase which is of central importance, e.g. *cats* in the phrase *my two, beautiful, Persian cats.* The head controls agreement with other sentence parts, e.g. *The cats were purring.*

heading

A title in the main body of a text that reflects the content of it. It may be left, centre or right justified in its position at the beginning of a text and techniques such as capitalisation or bold font may be used to draw the reader's attention to it.

hierarchy

An ordered system in which terms 'higher up' are made up of those immediately 'below', e.g. *sentence – clause - phrase – word – morpheme.*

high frequency words

Words needed most often by young writers and encountered most often in reading books. Because some of these words have irregular spellings, they need to be taught as **sight recognition words**, e.g. *said, come, was, you.* (See the National Literacy Strategy, pp. 60–1).

highlighting

Marking a text to make certain words or phrases stand out as an aid to comprehension.

home language

Language used at home.

homograph

Two words that are alike in spelling but have different meanings, e.g. *The wind blows. The blows caused serious bruising.* The pronunciation may be different, e.g. *bow (to bend down) and bow (used to fire an arrow).*

homonym
Two words originally from different sources that have merged into one, with identical spelling and pronunciation, but keeping their different meanings, e.g. *egg* meaning ovum and *egg* meaning to urge someone on.

homophone
Two words sounding the same, but with different spellings and meanings, e.g. *pain* (suffering) *pane* (plate of glass).

horror
A genre of children's books in which the subject is frightening, e.g. *Chills Run Down My Spine* by J. Vivelo, *Creepies (series)* by Rose Impey.

Activities for Writing Scary Stories (Thomas, 2001) are photocopiable activities and teacher guidance on the writing of scary stories.

hotseat

A **drama strategy** that involves questioning a person or group working in role.

hotspot
Part of a computer screen that the user clicks on to carry out a procedure.

HTML
Hyper-Text Mark-up Language — the language Internet documents are usually written in.

hyperlink
Underlined and often coloured blue, these are words in texts or parts of pictures that connect all parts of the World Wide Web.

hypertext
Computer text that has links.

hyphen
1. A **dash** used to join words together, e.g. *well-heeled*.

2. Another function of the hyphen is to mark words that have been divided by a line break.

hyponym
A word that can be included in the meaning of another larger category, e.g. *beech, oak, ash*/ *tree*. See **superordinate**.

iambic pentameter
A rhythm scheme in poetry of five iambic feet per line, that is ten syllables

altogether in a pattern of unstressed then stressed syllable, e.g. *The king / is dead / and I / will have / his crown*. Shakespeare made use of iambic pentameter in his writing.

icon
A pictorial symbol found on a computer tool bar which gives access to specific functions or programs, e.g. **B** *to create bold font.*

ICT
Information and Communication Technology. The National Curriculum requires that by the end of Key Stage 2 children should be able to read a range of ICT-based texts for reference and information purposes. They should compose on screen and paper and make use of the planning and proofing tools in a word processor. See the National Curriculum programme of study for reading and writing and ICT in the Literacy Hour CD-Rom.

ideograph
A written sign that symbolises an idea, e.g. Chinese written symbols and the hieroglyphs of the Egyptian writing system.

idiolect
Personal speech behaviours and idiosyncracies.

idiom
A well-known phrase or saying whose meaning goes beyond the literal, e.g. *He'll have to pull his socks up.*

illustration
A picture in a book which represent facets of the story or text.

illustrator
The person who draws the pictures in a book, e.g. *Quentin Blake, Debi Gliori, Nick Butterworth, Mick Inkpen.*

image
A tangible or mental representation of an object or person.

imagery
Words in a text which create an imaginative visual picture in the mind of the reader.

imperative
The **mood** of the verb that uses the **base verb** form usually without a subject. It occurs in **directive** sentences when requesting, advising or instructing someone to do something, e.g. *Please help! Fold the paper in half.* Exclamation marks often follow this construction.

imperative mood
The **mood** of the verb that is used to express **directives,** e.g. *Wait there!*

improvisation
An unprepared and unscripted composition.

indefinite article
The words 'a' and 'an', which are **determiners**.

indefinite pronoun
A type of pronoun denoting quantity, e.g. *Someone came to see me; nobody spoke; anything goes!*

indentation
A punctuation mark that signals a new paragraph; the text is a number of spaces in from the edge of the page.

independent clause
A clause (also known as 'main') that makes sense and can stand alone.

independent work/independent activities
Work carried out in the literacy hour without adult support: usually comprises 20 minutes.

Special Needs Literacy Resources for Group Time *from Scholastic are teacher resources for lower attainers, including lesson plans and photocopiable teachers' books for word, sentence and text level independent group work in the literacy hour.*

index
An alphabetically ordered list of the main entries in a book with page references, placed at the back of the book.

indicative
The **mood** of the verb used in statements and questions to express a factual meaning, e.g. *The weather is fine today.*

indirect object
The receiver of the direct object that follows some verbs, e.g. *Bring the purse to me!*

indirect speech
Speech that is reported and not a presentation of the actual words used. Certain grammatical changes are needed to verb tense, pronouns, time and place references, and there are no speech marks, e.g. *They said that they would leave the next day.* This is a report of the following direct speech: '*We will leave tomorrow,*' *they said.*

individual reading

1. The process of reading to someone on a one-to-one basis and being supported, taught or assessed.

2. Reading undertaken by a pupil without peer or adult support. This is usually silent reading and may take place at school (see **ERIC**) or at home. Within the literacy hour, it may be to prepare for or to follow up other work.

industrial spy

In discussion this is a strategy whereby an individual visits groups to hear ideas which will be communicated to the class later.

inference

1. Understanding the meaning of an unfamiliar word from the context.

2. Gaining meaning from a text which is not explicitly stated. An inferential question about a text asks the reader to understand and make deductions from what is explicitly stated in the text, e.g. *What do you think is the author's intention at this point in the story?*

infinitive

The non-finite base verb form, e.g. *to speak.* A non-finite, as opposed to a **finite verb,** does not change in respect of tense or subject agreement. Other verb forms are derived from the infinitive.

inflection

An alteration to the end of a word that reflects differences in tense, number, case, person or other grammatical feature e.g. *loves/loved* (tense), *child/children* (number), *the girl's coat* (case), *I, you, we, they wait/he, she, it waits* (person), *cold colder/coldest* (grammatical comparison).

information retrieval

The acquisition of facts from electronic texts and other sources. The information is made easily accessible to readers through devices such as contents pages and glossaries in books, keywords, and the search and find facility on a computer screen.

information text

Non-fiction material which presents facts about a topic. If this is a book, diagrams and specific information retrieval devices may be included to assist the reader, e.g. *index.*

initial

The position of a letter at the beginning of a word as opposed to **medial** or **final.**

innovation-on-text

Use of a known text as the model for a different composition .

insertion

An editing convention which involves making an addition to a text.

instruction text

A chronologically ordered text type that tells the reader or listener how to achieve something. The grammatical features include a statement of the outcome, the equipment needed and a list of actions to be taken. Verb forms are imperative and connectives usually refer to time. Recipes are instructional texts.

integrated composition

A multimedia text whose total meaning is derived from all of the component parts: words, pictures and sound.

interactive

Involving active participation and oral contribution from learners. This is a feature of whole-class teaching in the literacy hour when teachers engage pupils in individual questioning, action games and paired oral work.

interjection

A spoken utterance or noise which expresses feeling, usually shown by an exclamation mark e.g. *Wow! Sshhh!*

internal rhyme

A rhyme occurring within a line of text, e.g. *granite-weathered tors and heathered moors meet and greet the eye.*

interrogative

The structure used in questions. This is usually different from the structure of statements in that the subject and verb may change places, and a question mark is needed at the end e.g. *Is he alive?*

interrogative pronoun

A type of pronoun used at the beginning of a question, e.g. *Which do you want? Who is the winner? Whom do you admire most? Whose are those? What is she doing?*

intertextuality

Explicit or subtle references in one text to other texts that create rich layers of meaning for readers. Writers often exploit these connections deliberately e.g. *The Stinky Cheeseman and Other Fairly Stupid Tales by Jon Scieszka and Lane Smith.*

intervention

A strategy whereby the teacher interrupts the learning process to support the pupil/s and prevent misconception arising either by questioning, modelling or the provision of extra resources. It can be used in individual, group or whole-class English teaching situations. See **teaching at the point of writing.**

intonation

The tuneful rise and fall in pitch which carries meaning and expresses emotion in speech.

intransitive

Without an object, referring to verbs that are complete by themselves, e.g. *to happen.*

introduction

The opening of a text or speech. Some typical features of an introduction to a story may be the setting, the time the story is set and who the characters are. Conventional story openers include formulaic lines such as *A long time ago; Once upon a time.*

inverted commas

Pairs of commas placed around **direct speech**. Another name for inverted commas is **speech marks**.

irregular

Having forms not predictable by rules. There are irregular noun plurals, e.g. *tooth/teeth* and many irregular verbs, e.g. *to go* which has these unpredictable forms: *went, gone.*

ITA

Initial Teaching Alphabet — a former method of teaching reading conceived in 1960 using additional symbols to the traditional 26 alphabetic letters. The purpose was to facilitate the reading process for young children by providing separate symbols for each sound.

italic

A font in printed text in which the letters slant forwards. In handwriting, italic script is written with a wide-nibbed pen which creates thick and thin strokes.

jargon

Language used by a particular group of people related to an academic field, profession or leisure interest; others outside the group may not understand it.

jigsaw

A collaborative learning strategy for finding out information about a topic and practising speaking and listening skills in a purposeful context. A class may be divided into small groups called home groups whose aim is to research aspects of a topic. Each member of each home group is allocated a specific aspect of the topic and then re-forms into groups with a member from each of the other home groups working on the same aspect. These new expert groups then research the aspects they are allocated. Finally each member returns to the home group to inform them of the information they have found. Thus all aspects of the topic are researched.

jingle

A short rhyming verse, easy to remember, that often occurs in advertisements.

joined writing

The National Curriculum refers to cursive writing as joined writing.

journal

1. A factual account of daily events or **diary.** This may be written by an imagined author but based on historical evidence used by a modern writer, e.g. *Pirate Diary: The Journal of Jake Carpenter by Richard Pratt.*

2. A dated record of developing thoughts and ideas which is used to chart learning over a period of time.

3. A learned publication which is published regularly.

See **spelling journal.**

kenning

A form of poem using compound words to avoid naming something directly, e.g.

whisker-twitcher
mood-switcher
wool-tangler
mouse-mangler
soft-purrer
bird-scarer
alley-prowler
night-yowler.

key

A list of symbols and their meanings. Found in non-fiction texts accompanying diagrams, maps and charts.

keyword

A word that sums up the central topic of a paragraph or small chunk of text.

key words

Sets of high frequency words which occur often in reading books and which children learn to read and write. Lists for children in each primary year are provided in the National Literacy Strategy framework for teachers.

kinaesthetic

Relating to the action of muscles and corresponding movement of the body and used in the expression 'kinaesthetic learning'. See **multisensory.**

KWL

What we KNOW, What we WANT to find out, What we have LEARNED: a simple grid on which to record basic research information. These notes can be used as the basis for writing.

label

A named part of a diagram.

labelling

A **DARTS** comprehension activity that involves marking words in a text for a specific purpose, e.g. *to link information such as all the adverbs relating to a certain verb*.

landscape

The format of a book or page of writing that is a rectangle viewed horizontally.

language

The use of sounds, gestures and written signs for human communication and thought. Language is specifically highlighted in the Areas of Learning in the Curriculum Guidance for the Foundation Stage: Communication, Language and Literature.

layout

The arrangement of illustration and text in a book and how these interrelate**.**

legend

A heroic story set in the past. There may be underlying truth to the story if it is based on a real-life character, e.g. *Arthur, High King of Britain by M.Morpurgo*. See **genre**.

letter

A grapheme or symbol in an alphabetic writing system that may be a vowel or consonant.

letter formation

The shape, size and orientation of letters and how to write them using the rules of **directionality**.

letter string

A pattern of two or three letters which often occur together in words, e.g str.

lexical set

A set of words linked in some way, such as spelling patterns or meaning. The members of a set are linked to the same topic or register, e.g. *deuce, let, serve, volley* refer to the **discourse** of tennis.

lexical word

A word that carries meaning which is often called a **content** word. Lexical words are constantly being added to the language, often imported from other languages, e.g. *Doppelgänger* (a double) from German, or are creations to accompany new technology, e.g. *emoticon*.

lexicology

The study of the words in a language.

lexicon

A dictionary.

lexis

The vocabulary or words in a language, generally content words.

library skills

The abilities that enable readers to make effective use of the library and its resources, *e.g. the Dewey decimal classification system, the books and electronic sources of information with their specific information retrieval devices.*

ligature

A small stroke that joins two letters in **cursive** script.

limerick

A humorous poem of five lines with rhyme scheme aabba and traditionally a rhythmic pattern of 88668 syllables, e.g.

> *There was a young student from Rye,*
> *Whose essays made her tutors cry*
> *She can't write a sentence*
> *Nor handle a verb tense*
> *A gloss(a)ry's the thing she should try.*

linear narrative

Writing with a beginning, middle and end that is read from left to right and top to bottom.

lingua franca

In multilingual countries this is a common language used in formal education.

linguistic features

The language aspects of a text or dialogue.

listening

An auditory skill that, alongside speaking, forms Attainment Target 1 in the English National Curriculum and is part of Communication, Language and Literature in the *Curriculum Guidance for the Foundation Stage* (QCA/DfEE, 2000).

The QCA document, *Teaching Speaking and Listening at Key Stages 1 and 2* (1999), provides valuable information and advice.

Word Games *(Puddick, 2001) from BBC Educational Publishing is an activity book for listening and spelling.*

literacy
Reading and writing.

Learning Targets for Literacy *from Stanley Thornes includes sections of structured lesson plans for teaching literacy at Key Stages 1 and 2.*

On Target English *(Frost et al., 2001) is an integrated skills-based pro-gramme aimed at boosting levels of attainment in English. It includes pu-pils' books, interactive big book and a teachers' resource book.*

literacy event
Any event involving reading or writing.

literacy hour
An hour in the school day when literacy is taught in a prescribed way accord-ing to the National Literacy Strategy.

100 Literacy Hours *from Scholastic includes plans and suggested re-sources and activities for teaching the literacy hour. There is one tea-cher's book for each of the primary years.*

literal
Exact in meaning, not metaphorical. A literal question about a text asks the reader about events, characters and objects described in the text and is a form of information retrieval, e.g. *What happened when Red Riding Hood entered her grandmother's house?*

literary text
1. A text type, often fiction, which is recognised as well-written and is va-lued for its quality.

2. Written in a style characterised by a figurative use of language. The Na-tional Curriculum requires pupils in Key Stage 2 to explore both literary and **non-literary texts**.

literature
Verse and prose compositions that make up a body of writing that is valued by society.

loan word
A word imported from another language and added to the English vocabulary, often because of the prestige attached to the foreign language. Some words are assimilated to the extent that their origins are hard to spot; others are obviously alien e.g. *tour de force* (feat of strength or skill in French). Many have unusual letter strings or pronunciations that signal their difference, e.g. *gymkhana (of Hindi origin)*. The contrasting initial sounds in vixen and fox are due to a dialect loan. The /v/ comes from a dialect of Kent. Sometimes, technical vocabulary used by a small group of people becomes common property, e.g. *in vitro fertilisation* is a loan from medicine.

log
A chronologically organised text charting events and progress made, e.g. *a spelling log*.

logogram
A symbol standing for a word or words, e.g. *@*.

look and say
An approach to the teaching of reading based on visual recognition of whole words, sometimes learned by heart from **flashcards**.

lower case
Writing using letters which are not capitals (upper case).

main clause
The most important **clause** in a sentence having a **subject** and **verb** in agreement. It is the clause which is independent and not **subordinate**, e.g. *He likes to paint portraits* because people interest him.

major sentence
A sentence that is constructed in a regular way with a predictable pattern of elements. Major sentences may be **simple** or **multiple.**

mantle of the expert
A **drama strategy** whereby pupils adopt the role of a character with expertise and knowledge.

mapping
Pictorial presentation of an idea or topic in diagrammatic form, e.g. *mapping out elements or events in a story.*

mass noun
A **common noun** that refers to an amount rather than countable items, e.g. *sugar, poverty.* See **noun**.

matching
Pairing items that correspond, such as a letter with a particular sound or a picture with a word.

medial
The position of the middle **grapheme** or **phoneme** in a word, *e.g. the letter 'a' in 'cat'; the phoneme /o/ in 'pot'.* Usually refers to a **vowel**.

medium frequency word
A word which may be easily read but problematic to write because of irregular spelling. Such words are taught through years 4 and 5 and are identified in List 2 in the **National Literacy Strategy, p 62.**

menu
Drop down list of functions from icons or words on a computer tool bar.

metacognition
Awareness of one's own thoughts and thinking processes and the ability to reflect on them.

metalanguage
Specific vocabulary with which to talk about language and linguistic ideas, e.g. *sentence, cohesion.*

metaphor
Figurative language in which one thing is described as if it were something else, e.g. *the rosy cheeks of the apple, a picture of health.* Sometimes a whole poem may be constructed with one long or extended metaphor, e.g. *The Sea* by James Reeves.

mime
The act of communicating with gesture and the body rather than the voice

mind-map
A form of note-making using a visual representation of the theme and related ideas. Links are made explicit by use of colour, symbols and individual words.

minor sentence
A sentence that is constructed in an irregular way and which does not have the normal clause elements. See diagram with **sentence**.

misconception
An incomplete or inaccurate understanding.

miscue

An error in a pupil's reading or spelling providing diagnostic information for a teacher.

miscue analysis

A diagnostic procedure by which a child's reading or spelling strategies are identified, thus enabling the teacher to plan for further practice in underused strategies.

mnemonic

A strategy to help you remember information, often spellings or facts, that often involves making up a rhyme or short sentence to represent the things to be learned, e.g. *'i' before 'e' except after 'c'.*

modal

An **auxiliary verb** that implies how the writer feels about a subject, whether it is desirable, possible or necessary, e.g. *can/could, may/might, shall/ should, must/ought, will/would.* Modals are followed by the **infinitive** verb form, e.g. *They must <u>leave</u>. They ought <u>to be</u> home.*

mode

The medium of communication, such as speech or writing.

modelling

A teaching strategy which involves an expert **demonstrating** to learners and talking out loud as he or she reads/writes so that thought processes are revealed to the listeners.

modify

To affect or change meaning by making something more specific and precise. **Adjectives** can modify nouns, e.g. *the <u>white</u> cliffs.* **Prepositional phrases** can modify nouns, e.g. *the man <u>in the moon.</u>* **Adverbs** can modify other adverbs e.g. *They spoke <u>terribly</u> quickly.* In composing written texts pupils are taught to interest the reader by careful choice of words, so that the content of the text is appropriate to audience and purpose. For instance pupils may be taught to select more **powerful verbs** than 'said', *e.g. whispered, bellowed, mumbled.*

The National Literacy Strategy document, Grammar for Writing (DfEE, 1999, p.10), provides information and support.

monolingual

Speaking one language.

monologue

A speech made by one person, sometimes called a soliloquy in a play.

monosyllabic
Having one syllable, e.g. *map, shoe.*

mood
The form of the verb as it relates to sentence meaning. See **imperative, indicative, subjunctive.**

moral
A message emanating from a text, often a story, that readers can reflect on and use as a model for conducting their lives in a certain way.

morpheme
The smallest unit of meaning in the hierarchy of grammar. Words that can stand alone are called free morphemes, while bound morphemes are tiny bits that can be added to words. Some are added to the beginning and are **prefixes**, e.g. *un*fortunate. Some are added to the end and are **suffixes**, e.g. the plural 's' ending in *book/books* and the *er* (comparative) and *est* (superlative) endings in *bold/bolder/boldest.*

morphology
The study of words and their component parts.

mother tongue
The language spoken in the home. It may be also written.

moving image text
In reading in Key Stage 2 pupils could support their study of literary texts by accessing moving image texts such as film, television and multi-media.

multicultural
Representing many cultures.

multilingual
Representing or speaking many languages.

multimedia
Combined use of different media: still and moving images, sound, speech and writing.

multimedia authoring
Creating a multimedia text from draft to final version.

multiple literacies
The many different ways of using and accessing texts which function in different social contexts or situations. Each can be considered situated literacy, e.g. *school literacy.*

multiple sentence
A sentence that can be analysed into more than one clause and which can be either **compound** or **complex**.

multisensory
A teaching approach that uses all the channels of sight, sound, touch and movement. The channels are sometimes called visual, auditory and kinaesthetic modes of learning. Children see, hear and write a word to reinforce reading and spelling.

myth
A story about heroes and their dealings with gods, fabulous creatures and monsters. There are human truths to be learned from these tales as well as understanding about the natural world and its creation, e.g. *Wanderings of Odysseus by R. Sutcliff.*

narrative
A chronological text, usually fictional, in which events are related from one or more viewpoints within a structure of beginning, middle and end. It may be written in prose or poetry.

narrator
The implicit or explicit presenter of a play or story. In first-person narratives the narrator may be the main character, e.g. *Black Beauty by Anna Sewell.* In third person narratives the narrator reports on events using the different characters' names or **personal pronouns**, e.g. *The Iron Man by Ted Hughes* and *Mr. Gumpy's Outing by John Burningham*

Cracking Good Books *(Graham, 1997) offers advice and information.*

narrative viewpoint
The perspective from which a story is related, for example that of an external narrator or from the view of one or more characters within the story.

National Curriculum
This document sets out the requirements for all curriculum subjects studied in the primary and secondary phases of education. The education of children in their early years is known as the Foundation Stage and is followed by Key Stages 1, 2, 3 and 4, when compulsory education ends. In the Foundation Stage 'Communication, Language and Literacy' is one of six curriculum areas and covers speaking and listening, reading and writing. Early Learning Goals set the expectations for most children to reach by the end of the Foundation Stage. In Key Stages 1 and 2 English is separated into three areas known as programmes of study: English 1 – speaking and listening; English 2 – reading; English 3 – writing. Each programme of study is divided into knowledge, skills and understanding and breadth of study, which are then sub-divided.

The attainment targets for English setting the expectations that most children should reach by the end of each Key Stage are set as eight different levels, but only the relevant six levels are presented in the Key Stage 1 and 2 documentation.

National Literacy Strategy (NLS)

A government-initiated strategy for teaching **literacy** in primary and secondary schools. This incorporates work at **word, sentence** and **text** levels.

Discovery World and Rhyme World from Heinemann are a range of big books and spiral bound large-format books representing different genres with large-format text and teacher notes. For children from 4 to 7+.

neologism

A new word or phrase or a word or phrase used in a new way.

non-chronological

Organised on a principle other than that of time sequence. A description, for instance of an object may start by placing the object in a general category, then list its attributes and note its function.

non-fiction

Information in text form that is true and based on actual fact.

Non-fiction Writing Frames for Infants (Harrison, 2000) is a useful teaching resource, as are the activity pack on non-fiction skills Junior Focus from Scholastic (1998/2000) and the posters provided in Stanley Thornes Primary Literacy (1999).

non-finite

A verb form that does not change in respect of **tense, number, person** or **mood**. The -ed and -ing **participles**, and the **base form** used as an infinitive are non-finite.

non-linear

Organised not as a conventional narrative with beginning, middle and end, nor read from left to right and top to bottom, but structured in a different way as in a **multimedia** composition

non-literary text

Text types which are often functional, non-fiction, written in a literal style with little use of figurative language, e.g. *recipes, reports*. The National Curriculum requires pupils at Key Stage 2 to explore both **literary** and non-literary texts.

non-narrative

Any text type which is not a story, e.g. *advertisements or instructions.*

non-restrictive clause

A **relative clause** giving extra information (that could be omitted) about a **head noun**. It is marked off with a pair of commas e.g., My son, <u>who lives in France,</u> arrives tomorrow. See **restrictive clause.**

non-verbal communication

Use of the body to communicate, *e.g. facial expressions and* **gestures.**

note making

Writing or recording the important information from a text or observed event in a shortened form, not using full sentences. This may involve omitting words which are not vital to the meaning, using diagrams or personal symbols to capture the main points of something read, heard or seen. See **note taking**.

note taking

See **note making.** In *Grammar for Writing* the terms **note making** and **note taking** are used interchangeably.

The National Literacy Strategy document Grammar for Writing (DfEE, 1999, pp. 58 and 140) provides information and guidance.

noun

A word class that denotes the names with which we refer to things. Nouns may be categorised as **proper** or **common**. Common nouns may be categorised as count or mass. Both these categories can be subdivided into **concrete** and **abstract.**

Noun Classes

```
                    Noun Classes
         ┌───────────────┴────────────────┐
      proper                            common
      England                           country
                                ┌──────────┴──────────┐
                              mass                   count
                         ┌──────┴──────┐        ┌──────┴──────┐
                     abstract     concrete   abstract    concrete
                       luck         milk       joy         book
```

noun phrase

A group of words with a central or **head** noun that controls agreement with other sentence parts, e.g. *My brilliant young nephew from York writes regularly.* The head noun and the **determiner** make up a simple noun phrase, *my nephew,* which controls the choice of verb *writes*. The head noun with other modifiers, *my brilliant young nephew from York,* is known as a complex noun phrase.

novel
A book of fictional narrative writing in prose, usually organised in chapters.

novella
A short novel.

number

The system of choice in grammar between **singular** and **plural**.

obituary
A text written as an announcement or an evaluation of the life of someone who has recently died.

object
One of the elements of the **clause** which denotes what has been affected by the action of the **verb**. In statements, the object follows the verb, as in *I ate my packed lunch*. An object may be direct as in *my packed lunch*, which is the thing given, or indirect as in *The cook gave me a packed lunch*, where *me* means *to me*. *Verbs followed by a direct object are termed* **'transitive'**.

ode
A poem meant to be sung or one directly addressing a person or thing and written in a lyrical style, *e.g. Ode to the North-East Wind by Charles Kingsley, Ode on the Death of a Favourite Cat Drowned in a Tub of Gold Fishes by Thomas Gray.*

omission
A spelling error whereby letters are missed out e.g. *ther (their)*. In reading young children may sometimes omit words. In **miscue analysis** this may be noted.

onomatopoeia
The formation of a word which imitates the sound of the thing it represents, e.g. *clatter, ping, cuckoo*.

onset
The initial consonant part of a syllable, e.g. *cat, but*. Some words have no onset, e.g. *end, ant*. Used in the phrase 'onset and rime'. See **rime.**

opinion
The personal view of a speaker or writer, which contrasts with factual information. In the National Curriculum pupils are required to discriminate in their reading between what is true and what may be a biased representation of events. In speaking and listening pupils give their opinions and justify them.

oracy
This is termed 'speaking and listening' in the National Curriculum.

orientation
1. In handwriting the arrangement of letters in space.

2. In story structure the opening section which introduces characters and sets the scene.

oronym
A string of sounds that can be broken up into words in two different ways producing difference in meaning, e.g. *ice cream, I scream.*

orthography
The study of the conventions of spelling within a writing system.

overgeneralisation
Creating language by using a known rule which, because there are exceptions to the rule, sometimes results in young children making errors e.g. *I writed my name today.* The rule for adding 'ed' to the base verb to make the past tense is overgeneralised because the child is, as yet, unaware of the irregular past form 'wrote'.

paired reading
A strategy whereby an experienced reader is paired with a less experienced one so that peer teaching and support may take place.

palindrome
A word or phrase that reads the same from left to right as right to left, e.g. *Hannah.*

parable
A story whose purpose is to teach a moral lesson. Parables may be written in prose or verse. They can be found in the Bible, e.g. *The Parable of the Old Men and the Young* by Wilfred Owen.

paragraph
A chunk of text comprising several sentences related to one key idea.

parentheses
A pair of brackets, equivalent to a pair of commas or dashes, that is placed around an explanation or elaboration inserted into a sentence. The inserted expression is known as a parenthesis, e.g. *Lavender and rosemary (herbs that love dry, sandy soils) are very aromatic.*

parody
A humorous imitation or exaggeration of a text in terms of its style, linguistic

features or structure.

participle

A form of the verb made by adding either 'ing' or 'ed' to the base **verb**.

The 'ing' form is sometimes known as a present participle, though it is not restricted to present time; it can express the continuous past, e.g. *She was leaving*. It can also function as a noun (known formerly as a **gerund),** e.g. *Swimming is a healthy type of exercise*. Adding 'ing' often involves a spelling change e.g. *hop + ing = hopping*.

The *ed* form is known as a past participle, but is not restricted to past time. It is used with 'have' to make the present perfective aspect, e.g. *They have landed*. It is used after *be* to make the passive, e.g. *I am wounded*. The 'ed' ending often results in spelling changes and pronunciation differences, e.g. *hoped, tried, faded*. Some verbs have irregular past participles, e.g. *see/seen, sleep/slept*.

parts of speech

An older term for **word classes**. In the National Curriculum programme of study for reading pupils are required to learn word classes and the grammatical functions of words, including nouns, verbs, adjectives, adverbs, pronouns, prepositions, conjunctions and articles.

passive voice

Relating to the **verb** in a sentence where the object is moved to the beginning and given a subject function e.g. *The seeds were eaten by the birds* uses the passive voice. The agent is sometimes omitted, e.g. *The seeds were eaten*.

*The birds **ate** the seeds* uses the **active** voice.

The passive voice is used more in writing than speech.

The passive is a common construction in writing of certain genres, *e.g. reports,* or when the agent needs to be excluded.

past tense

One of the tenses in English. Past tense refers to events that happened in the past, e.g. *She visited her cousin last week*. There are 2 forms – simple 'he danced' progressive 'he was dancing'. Usually, 'ed' is added to the **base verb** form to make the past, e.g. *arrive/arrived, scream/screamed*. Some verbs have less regular forms, e.g. *go/went, take/took*. See **aspect**.

perfective

One of the two types of **aspect** (the other being *progressive*) which shows whether the action denoted by the verb is complete, is in progress or is of a certain duration. There are two perfective forms: present and past and both use the auxiliary of the verb 'to have'. The present perfective denotes an action that carries on up to the present, e.g. *I <u>have lived</u> in Winchester for almost* *a year.* The past perfective suggests a similar meaning but refers to a duration up to a point in the past, e.g. *He was upset that he <u>had received</u> no invitation to the meeting.*

person

In grammar the difference between first person *I/we*, 2nd person *you*, third person he/she/they/it. In some instances, the form of the verb changes according to person, as in *I <u>am</u>, you/we /they <u>are</u>, he/she/it <u>is</u>.* Certain text types are characterised by the use of a specific person, e.g. *first person use in a diary or recount.*

personal pronoun

A word that identifies who is speaking, writing or being addressed, e.g. *I/me, he/him, she/her, we/us, they/them.*

personification

A metaphor in which something non–human is given human attributes and described accordingly, e.g. *a shrill wind screaming, the thick fog menacing.*

persuasive text

A text whose purpose is to gain support for a particular belief or cause. Its structure comprises a statement of the point of view, followed by justified arguments. Opposing views and supporting evidence may also be included. It concludes with a summary or recommendation. Linguistic features include connectives, e.g. *therefore, however, all in all, in other words.* An essay on banning smoking would be an example of this text type.

phoneme

The smallest unit of sound which makes a difference in meaning, e.g. *cat, hat.* Phonemes are often signalled in writing by the use of slashes, e.g. */b/.* There are about 44 phonemes in English and some are pronounced differently according to their position in a word, e.g. *final /l/ in full is different from initial / l/ in light.* One phoneme may be represented by one or more letters e.g. *mat-/m/, think-/th/, thought-/au/.* The same letters may represent more than one phoneme e.g. *bead- /ee/ deaf-/e/.* The same phoneme may be represented in writing in more than one way e.g. */ae/ - day, rain, take.* See entries **vowel phoneme** and **consonant phoneme**.

The National Literacy Strategy document Progression in Phonics (DfEE, 2000) offers information and support.

phonetics

The study of speech sounds, how they are articulated, transmitted and perceived.

phonics

A term commonly used to denote an approach to the teaching of reading in which children are taught sound–letter correspondence.

Soundstart from Stanley Thornes are large-format flipover books with laminated pages for whole-class or group teaching of phonics. Each page contains a picture with several items beginning with a letter of the alphabet and a section for practising writing the alphabet letters.

Jolly Phonics from Jolly Learning, Spelling and Phonics from Scholastic and Phonicability from Hopscotch are also useful resources.

phonology
The study of the sound system of a particular language.

phonological awareness
Sensitivity to sounds in words and the ability to segment and blend them.

phrasal verb
A verb combined with one or more prepositions or adverbs forming a verb phrase with a particular meaning which is different from the meanings of the individual parts, *e.g. give in, shut up, get on with, look after (care for).*

phrase
A group of words acting together within a clause. A phrase can function as a noun, e.g. _The red butterfly_ landed. It can function as an adjective, e.g._That's very unfortunate,_ or an adverb e.g. _He walked really slowly._ **A prepositional phrase** can function as an adjective, e.g. _the cat with long fur_ or an adverb e.g. _arriving on Thursday._ See **noun phrase**, **adjectival phrase** and **adverbial phrase**.

pictograph
A sign derived from a picture of an object. Pictographs were used in some early writing systems and are found in modern Mandarin script.

picture cue
The information in pictures which may help with reading and interpreting a text.

picture books
Texts where illustration plays a central role in the telling of the story or presentation of facts. Picture books without words are sometimes called **sequenced picture texts**. They demand **visual literacy** skills from readers.

picture planning
A compositional tool involving drawing a series of pictures representing events in a story or chronological account. A short text may be added beneath.

plan

To develop and note initial ideas for a piece of writing; this process may use ideas previously discussed in **talk for writing**. In shared writing pupils are taught how to translate their plans into written texts.

The National Literacy Strategy document Developing Early Writing (DfEE, 2001, pp.14–16) offers information and support.

play

An improvised or scripted drama that is designed to be acted out.

playscript

A written text type involving characters, dialogue and plot whose purpose is to entertain, inform or educate.

plenary

The concluding part of a literacy or other lesson which may be used for assessment or review of what has been learned, for addressing misconceptions, for groups to explain their work or for the teacher to prepare for follow-up lessons.

plot

The events and the causal links between them that create what happens in a story.

plural

The plural form of a word indicates that there is more than one. It is usually signalled by an 's' ending e.g. *glove/gloves*. Some words form the plural irregularly e.g. *child/children*, or change some letters before adding 's' *e.g. wife/wives*.

poem

A text that may have a recognisable **form**, **rhyme** and **rhythmic** pattern. Poetic language is often **figurative**, with ideas condensed for maximum impact. Prose may achieve the same effect.

poetry

An oral or written genre that often makes use of **figurative language**, rhythm and rhyme patterns and has a familiar structure e.g. *sonnet, haiku*. In poetry, words are selected carefully and the meaning is often highly condensed. Prose and poetry are sometimes considered as opposites, but they both lie along a continuum; prose can be poetic in the way it is written and poetry can be written with the sound of prose.

From the earliest stage of education and throughout the primary years, poetry is a genre that pupils are required, in the English National Curriculum, to read and later to write.

polysyllabic
Having many **syllables**, e.g. *chronological, indicative, recuperating.*

polysemy
A **semantic** term for the process whereby the meaning of a single word is extended, sometimes **metaphorically**, e.g. *tongue* (1) *of body* (2) *of shoe.*

portmanteau
A word fused from parts of two others, e.g. *smog (smoke + fog), brunch (breakfast + lunch).*

portrait
Book or page format that is like a rectangle with its longest sides in a vertical position.

possessive pronoun
A kind of **pronoun** showing ownership. There are two forms: *my, your, her,* etc., that function as determiners within a noun phrase, e.g. *my house, their garden;* the second form includes *mine, his, ours, its* etc., which stand alone, e.g. *This is yours.* The only possessive pronoun in this second group to take an apostrophe is *'one',* e.g. *One should stick to* <u>*one's*</u> *principles.*

powerful verb
A stylistic choice in vocabulary, involving a precise **verb** which will make an impact on a reader, e.g. *shuffled, sauntered, strutted* instead of *moved.* See **modify.**

predicate
The part of a sentence that comes after the **subject**, e.g. *The postman* <u>*dropped the letters.*</u>

prediction
An intelligent guess based on previous language experience and implicit grammatical knowledge that readers use as they interpret a text and anticipate what comes next.

prefix
An affix added to the front of a **root** word to make a new word with a different meaning, e.g. <u>*un*</u>*happy.* Prefixes are **derivational morphemes.**

preposition
One of the main **word classes**. The main function of **prepositions** e.g. *over, on, at, of, to, with,* is to indicate time, position or direction e.g. *My colleague left school* <u>*at*</u> *5 o'clock. Then she drove* <u>*to*</u> *the meeting.*

prepositional phrase
A group of words, often a **noun phrase**, that follow a **preposition**, together

with the preposition itself, e.g. *I found the pen <u>under the table</u>*. In this example, the prepositional phrase is functioning as an **adverbial**.

present

To present is to prepare a neat, correct, final copy of a written text. This is part of the writing process specified in the National Curriculum programme of study for writing at Key Stage 2.

present tense

A **verb** form that usually relates to time now e.g. *The bird is <u>flying</u> in the air.* The present may also be used with repeated events e.g. *I <u>swim</u> every week.* It also denotes an event outside of time *e.g. 3 x 4 is 12.* Other times may also be shown by the present tense, e.g. *They arrive tonight* (future). There are two forms of the present tense: present simple, e.g. *He flies* and present progressive, e.g. *He is flying.* See **aspect**.

presentation

1. The appearance of a piece of work and how it strikes the eye.

2. The showing of work to an audience, which may be evaluated and assessed.

print

A style of handwriting in which each letter is separate from the next.

Some schools teach young children handwriting using print and others begin with **cursive** script.

procedural text

A chronological text whose purpose is to help the reader succeed in doing or making something, e.g. *a recipe.* The structure may comprise a statement of the outcome, the items needed to achieve this and an ordered list of actions to be taken. Connectives of time and imperative verb forms feature in this text type. Procedural means the same as **instructional.**

pro-form

A word which stands in for another, sometimes longer, construction, e.g. *I've got a new bike and my sister's got <u>one</u>, too.*

progressive

One of the two types of **aspect** (the other being *perfective*) that is also called *continuous.* It is used with both tenses and both perfective aspects. It is constructed with the verb 'be' + ing verb form and denotes an event taking place at a particular time that is not necessarily finished e.g. *I <u>am swimming</u>, they <u>were skating</u>, we <u>have been running</u>, she <u>had been cycling</u>.* Forms that are not progressive are called 'simple' and these emphasise the completeness of the event e.g. *I <u>ran</u> a race* (past simple) or *They <u>had driven</u> in the rally.* (past perfective simple).

pronoun
One of the main word classes. It can replace a noun. See **personal pronoun, reflexive pronoun, possessive pronoun** relative.

proofread
To check work carefully before making a final version.

prose
Speech or writing that is not in verse. Though for everyday purposes it usually does not contain **figurative language,** prose may be poetic just as some poetry may be prosaic.

prosody
Loudness, pitch, tempo and rhythm, which play a role in speech similar to that of punctuation in writing.

proverb
An old saying expressing a belief or common sense view derived from experience, e.g. *Every cloud has a silver lining.*

pun
A play on words intended to amuse. A word is used in a way that evokes more than one meaning or a similar sounding word with a different meaning is used. Advertising jingles and newspaper headlines often involve puns as they catch the reader's attention e.g. *Railways on track at last!* Punning was a device popular with Elizabethan writers, e.g. In Macbeth, II.ii, Lady Macbeth plots to incriminate the guards in Duncan's murder; her word 'guilt' plays on the word 'gilt' meaning 'gold coating'.

> *If he do bleed,*
> *I'll gild the faces of the grooms withal,*
> *For it must seem their guilt.*

Humorous poets, e.g. *Ogden Nash, Edward Lear* and *Lewis Carroll* use punning in their verse for children.

punchline
A culminating or concluding point in speech or writing (often in joke or humorous anecdote) which makes a great impact on the audience and releases the tension that has been built up.

punctuation
A system of marks used in writing to define grammatical boundaries and to serve a role similar to **stress** and **intonation** in speech. It is an aid to the reader's understanding. At Key Stage 1 pupils are taught capital letters, full stops and question marks and begin to use commas. In addition, at Key Stage 2, they are taught exclamation marks, inverted commas and apostrophes.

The Punctuation Show CD Rom from Sherston Software is a great resource for teaching punctuation with Key Stage 2 children.

purpose

The motivation for producing a text, oral or written. The linguistic choices that
speakers or writers make will be influenced not only by their intended audience but by their purpose. A text that sets out to persuade will be shaped
structurally and linguistically in a very different way from one whose main
purpose is to entertain, for example.

QUADS

Question, Answer, Details, Source — this is a matrix on which to record research information in a structured way.

quattrolinear

A script written between four lines to accommodate **ascenders** and **des-
cenders**, e.g. *English*.

question mark

A **punctuation mark** placed at the end of an **interrogative** sentence, e.g.
May I leave now?

questioning

A professional language practice that may be used in speech or writing to
elicit information and ideas, and to develop or assess understanding.

rainbow

A technique used to practise speaking and listening skills that involves all
members of a group visiting other groups as **envoys** in order to pool and
extend ideas.

range

In English in the National Curriculum this refers to the diversity of texts that
pupils should have opportunities to read and write.

rap

A form of oral poem that has a strong rhythm and fast tempo. Grace Nichols,
John Agard, James Berry and Benjamin Zephaniah write poetry that often
involves rapping. It is usually from Black poetry and is linked with pop music.

reading

The requirements for the teaching of reading at Key Stages 1 and 2 are laid
out in the National Curriculum English programmes of study (En 2), which
specify the knowledge, skills, understanding and breadth of study.

reading aloud

Sounding out a text either individually or in a group. Teachers read aloud to pupils in order to **model** certain skills. By listening, pupils absorb the rhythms of language and vocabulary which can be recreated in their own writing. Sometimes teachers listen to pupils reading aloud in order to assess their understanding.

reading conference

An informal assessment procedure which involves a dialogue between teacher and pupil. The discussion may highlight pupils' attitudes to reading as well as providing information about books read.

reading log

An individual record and evaluation of books read.

reading recovery

An intervention programme providing a period of intensive reading practice to those most at risk of failure. This idea was originally conceived by Clay (1979).

reading schemes

Published sets of reading books which are graded in difficulty.

The Book Project from Longman is a graded reading scheme for children from age 4 to 12, including graded books on different fiction and non-fiction genres, teachers' resource books, photocopiable masters, audio and video cassettes.

reading strategy

A method which a reader may use to decode text. A proficient reader uses a range of strategies. See National Literacy Strategy **searchlights model**.

recite

To say aloud a poem or piece of writing which has been learned by heart.

recount

A written **genre** whose purpose is to inform and entertain in retelling. It may be fictional with characters, dialogue and setting. If it is **non-fictional**, as in a **biography**, events may be told in **chronological** order.

reference

A type of text usually organised alphabetically that is used for **information retrieval**, e.g. *telephone directory.*

reflexive pronoun

A type of **pronoun** that always ends in 'self' or 'selves' which emphasises the meaning of a **noun** or **pronoun** in the sentence, e.g. *We kept it to ourselves.*

register
A socially created and recognised form of language used in a specific social situation.

regular verb
A **verb** that has predictable forms that are governed by rules. There are four forms for each regular verb: the base or infinitive, the -s form, the -ed form and the -ing participle e.g. *to listen/listens/listened/listening*. See **irregular.**

rehearse
To practise a skill that will help with a subsequent task such as reading a sentence out loud before writing it down.

relative clause
A type of **clause** that gives information about a **noun** or **noun phrase** and begins with a **relative pronoun**, e.g. *I knew the boy who was missing*. See **restrictive** and **non-restrictive** clauses.

relative pronoun
A type of **pronoun** used to link a relative clause to the **head** noun in a **phrase**, e.g. *who, whom, whose, which, that.* e.g. *I bought the book which had been serialised on the radio; This is the film that received all the accolades.*

renga
A complete series of poems comprising several **haiku** which may be written by different poets. Each haiku is linked to the next by two lines each of seven **syllables**.

reorganisation
A **comprehension** task involving locating information in a text and changing it, e.g. *a summary.*

report
A **non-chronological** text whose purpose is to classify or describe, e.g. *Farming in Ancient Egypt*. The structure involves a general classification, followed by a description of specific attributes with a final summary. The **tense** used is often the **present** continuous and the subjects are non-specific, e.g. *people, they, rivers.*

resolution
In terms of story structure this is when a problem that has formed an integral part of the **plot** is finally resolved.

response partner
Someone who will act as a critical friend and give feedback on your writing

or contribute to paired discussion in planning for writing or a talk task.

restrictive clause

A **relative clause** which limits the **noun** and is not marked off with commas, e.g. *My son who lives in France arrives tomorrow.* The clause 'who lives in France' restricts the noun 'son' to the one mentioned here. See **non-restrictive clause.**

retell

To tell a story in your own words without the original text.

review

1. A critical evaluation of a book or text.

2. An evaluation of progress made to date and setting of new goals.

revise

To improve a piece of writing in terms of **vocabulary**, **style** and structure.

rheme

The part of a sentence following the **theme.** The rheme does not have such prominent information as the theme.

rhetorical expression

An utterance whose intended meaning is not to be taken **literally** by the listener. In the example *Would you like to get out your exercise books now?* what is expressed as a question is perceived as a command by children in a classroom used to this language convention.

rhyme

1. The **stressed vowel phoneme** and following sounds in a word that sound like those in another, e.g. *say/play, teacher/creature.*

2. A short poem as in 'nursery rhyme', e.g. *Twinkle Twinkle Little Star by Jane Taylor*.

rhythm

The light and heavy beats (**stress** patterns) that recur in speech or music.

riddle

A puzzle, sometimes in rhyme, that requires a solution. Riddles, nursery rhymes and playground chants are part of a long-established oral tradition which has been researched by the folklorists Iona and Peter Opie and this work can be found in their classic text, *The Lore and Language of Schoolchildren* (1959). Some modern poetry collections are based on their work e.g. *Playground Treasury by Pie Corbett.*

rime

The **vowel** and final **consonant**(s) of a **syllable**, e.g. Examples of one syllable words are *pan, set* and *shop*.

role play

Adopting the role of a character to experience what it is like to feel, think and act from within that persona.

root

A term in **morphology** denoting the primary part of a word from which other words may be derived e.g. <u>*appear*/*appearance, apparently, disappeared.*</u>

RP

Received Pronunciation — an English accent perceived as **standard** and prestigious by some.

rule

In grammar, an underlying principle which is implicitly known by language users. Young children inherently know some of the rules of English, but often **overgeneralise** and produce non-standard utterances, e.g. *He's gooder than me.*

running record

An informal and diagnostic assessment technique that gives information about the **reading strategies** children use. The teacher has a copy of the text a child is reading and annotates it by adding marks or symbols against each word read. It is a simplified version of **miscue analysis**. This form of assessment is used in the National Curriculum Standard Assessment Tasks to ascribe a level of attainment in reading to individual pupils.

running story

Characters appearing throughout picture books who have no part to play in the main story and whose presence is not mentioned in the text.

scaffolding

A process by which learners are supported by adult **intervention** and appropriately presented tasks while aiming for independence.

scale

The relative size of elements in an illustration. In creating visual images to accompany stories writers and illustrators can give messages about the relative importance of certain elements through manipulating scale.

scan

1. To read for specific details only, a process similar to picking out a familiar face in a crowd.

2. To analyse the rhythmic structure of a line of poetry.

schwa

The neutral **vowel** sound which occurs in weakly stressed syllables, e.g. *com-panion, about*.

science fiction

A **genre** in which imagined worlds and their inhabitants figure prominently. Children's writers include Terry Pratchett, Robert Swindells and Julia Jarman.

Activities for Writing Sci-Fi Stories (Merchant, 2001) *includes photo-copiable activities and teacher guidance for whole class and group teaching.*

scribing

A writing process where someone records what is spoken. It is an important early stage in teaching writing with young children when the teacher writes down what they compose orally.

script

1.   A form of handwriting e.g. *cursive script*.

2.   Written notes forming an aide-memoire.

3.   The written text of a play.

searchlight

1.   A strategy used in reading and writing a text.

2.   The searchlights model in the National Literacy Strategy, p. 4:

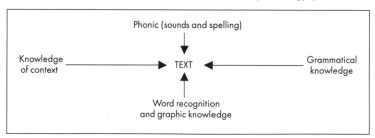

second language speaker

A person who speaks two languages, though not necessarily to the same level of competence.

segment

1.   To segment phonemically is to break down a word into its component phonemes.

2.   To say all the sounds in a word as an aid to spelling.

The National Literacy Strategy document Progression in Phonics (DfEE, 2000, p.4) offers information and support.

semantic

Relating to meaning. Children may use semantic strategies to decode unknown words when reading. They may ask whether it makes sense.

semi-colon

A punctuation mark which may be used between two clauses, though with the intention to signal a link between them, e.g. *I liked the film; it was an accurate portrayal of that period in history.* The semi-colon may separate items in a list if they are long phrases, e.g. *I bought two wholemeal loaves; 200 g of coarsely grated parmesan cheese; a tin of Spanish tuna in olive oil and a large bulb of organically grown garlic.*

semi-cursive

A style of handwriting in which some of the letters are not joined, e.g. *y, p, b, j, g.*

sentence

A unit in grammar above the **clause** which can stand independently and has a completed meaning. **Major sentences** follow regular grammatical rules and occur most frequently in writing. **Minor sentences** are irregular in construction and are usually found in speech.

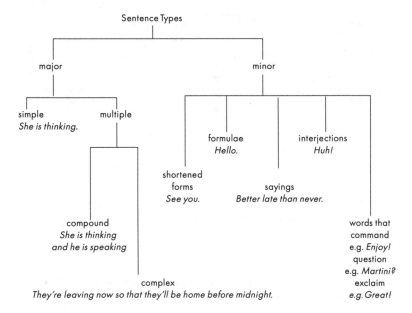

sentence level

National Literacy Strategy term for work relating to grammar and punctuation.

Words at Work (Phenix, various) are useful word and sentence level workbooks.

sequel

A text that follows on from another usually to bring the first text to a conclusion.

sequence

To arrange pictures or text in order so that there are links between the parts, which is a **comprehension** activity. See **DARTS**.

sequenced picture text

A text comprising pictures but no words. Jane Doonan in *Looking at Pictures in Picture Books* (1993) prefers this to 'wordless picture books'.

serial

A story that is published in instalments.

series fiction

Books with similar plots and characters, sometimes written by the same author, e.g. *The Internet Detectives by M. Coleman.*

setting

The environment in which a story takes place. Often this contributes significantly to the mood of the writing, e.g. *Storm by Kevin Crossley-Holland.* Setting may be part of characterisation in a novel or may give a very real sense of place and geographical location, e.g. *Journey to Jo'burg by B. Naidoo; Mufaro's Beautiful Daughters by J. Steptoe.*

shape poem

A poem in which shape is used to embody and enhance the meaning of the poem, e.g. *material in The Upside Down Frown by Andrew Fusek Peters.*

shared reading

Part of the literacy hour devoted to teaching reading with the whole class. The teacher **models** the reading process by reading a text to the pupils, which they would find too difficult to read independently. The support given by teacher and peers may enable pupils to join in.

Focus English *is a big book anthology from Reed Educational.*

shared writing

A strategy for teaching writing with the whole class. It currently takes place in the context of the literacy hour. The National Literacy Strategy proposes that teachers use shared reading or shared writing techniques every day in the first part of the literacy hour. It involves teaching **text level work** and using **sentence** and **word level work** in the context of **composing** a text. The teacher's role is first to **demonstrate** or model how a text is written. The focus is on demonstrating the process of composition explicitly. In subsequent whole-class shared writing sessions teachers may scribe for the pupils, encouraging them to compose and contribute ideas for parts of the text. The next stage is for pupils to undertake **supported composition** alone or with a partner to practise writing a small part of the text using a dry wipe board. The ultimate aim is for children to write independently. (See National Literacy Strategy document *Developing Early Writing*, DfEE, 2001, pp. 13–17.)

Here's One I Wrote Earlier (Matthews and Howell, 2002) offer time-saving photocopiable writing examples to use in modelled and shared writing sessions.

Pelican Shared Writing: Fiction and Non Fiction Resource Books from Pearson Educational are two big books with a range of fiction and non-fiction texts for whole-class text/genre work, accompanied by teachers' books. Writers' World (2001) by Heinemann provides source material for teachers to use with 7–11 year olds.

sight recognition word

A word occurring frequently in early reading books. Some sight words are tricky to write because their spellings are hard to predict. Pupils from Reception to Year 2 are taught to recognise them as whole words, usually in context, but other learning strategies may also be used. See List 1 in the National literacy Strategy, p. 60.

silent reading

Reading to oneself, the most natural behaviour of a reader.

simile

A form of **figurative** language in which a direct comparison is made using the words 'like' or 'as'. Some similes are well-used expressions, e.g. *as cold as ice.*

simple sentence

A sentence comprising one **clause**, e.g. *It was raining*. There must be a subject and a verb.

single language book

A book written in one language.

singular

Part of the number system in grammar which contrasts with **plural** and refers to single items e.g. *child/children; I/we; dog/dogs.*

skim
To read in order to understand the gist of a text.

skywriting
Large letters made in the air in order to practise **directionality** and shape through large body movements.

slang
An informal, often short–lived form of language, whose use may be a sign of group belonging. It is considered to be a non–standard rather than **standard** form of English.

snowball
A strategy used to practise speaking and listening skills whereby two people discuss an issue before joining with another pair to share ideas. The process of enlarging groups may continue.

sociolect
A class or regional **dialect**.

sonnet
A poem in which one idea is developed in one verse of 14 lines. The lines are usually **iambic pentameters** rhyming according to a fixed pattern. Shakespeare and Milton often wrote in sonnet form, e.g. *Shakespeare's Sonnet no. 18 'Shall I compare thee to a summer's day?' is an example of the customary Elizabethan sonnet rhyme scheme: abab cdcd efef gg.*

sound
A tone produced by regular vibrations of the vocal chords as air passes through them.

Early readers are taught to hear the sounds in words when learning to read. These individual sounds are **phoneme**s. There are **consonant** and **vowel phonemes**. This phonemic knowledge helps young readers to decode and spell regular words.

space
A **punctuation** mark to signal an interval or boundary between words or lines of text.

speaking and listening
the requirements for the teaching of speaking and listening at Key Stages 1 and 2 are laid out in the National Curriculum Programmes of Study for English (En1), which specify the knowledge, skills, understanding and breadth of study.

Word Games (Puddick, 2001) from BBC Educational is an activity book for listening and spelling.

speech

Oral language used for many purposes, particularly to maintain social relationships, and which may have a grammar different from that of written English.

speech bubble

A presentational device in an illustrated text showing characters' actual words framed in a 'bubble' coming out of the mouth and replacing the speech marks normally used in dialogue.

speech marks

Pairs of commas placed around a speaker's original words in a text. This type of speech is called **direct speech** and the commas mark the beginning and end of the spoken words, e.g. *"We're late,"* my friend said. Another name for speech marks is **inverted commas**.

spelling

Producing the **graphemic** form of a word with its constituent letters. Children may use **phonemic** information, graphical and whole-word knowledge in spelling words.

All of these resources are useful for teaching spelling: The Spelling Show CD Rom (Sherston Software), Spelling and Phonics (Reeve, 1998), I Love Spelling CD Rom (Dorling Kindersley) and the Finger Spelling Alphabet poster (BBC Educational).

spelling log

An individual list of words needing to be learned.

spelling journal

A self-help tool for the pupil containing an individual list of words needing to be learned together with other helpful material e.g. **mnemonics,** *words derived from given roots.*

The National Literacy Strategy document Spelling Bank (National Centre for Literacy and Numeracy, 1999, p.76) offers support and information.

spidergram

A note-making technique involving writing down a central idea with links displayed around it.

spine
The strong, left-hand edge of a book into which the pages are bound.

split digraph
Two vowels separated by a consonant making one **phoneme**, e.g. fame/ael, hide/ie, drove/oe.

split narrative
In picture books when one setting is used as background for two events involving different characters.

spokesperson
A role within a group that entails gathering group ideas and reporting back to a wider audience on the group's behalf.

standard English
A non-regional variety of English which exists in spoken and written form and which has prestige as a medium of communication. It can be spoken with any accent. It is a form specified in the English National Curriculum and taught in primary schools. Other varieties of English may have different grammar and vocabulary. Several English-speaking countries have their own standard forms, e.g. *American English*.

standardised test
An assessment technique, often used for spelling or reading, which gives a numerical score, enabling national comparisons to be made between individuals tested. This sort of test is norm referenced as opposed to criterion referenced.

stanza
A unit of poetry comprising a verse or series of lines whose pattern is repeated throughout the poem.

statement
A sentence type whose purpose is to give information. There is a **subject** followed by a **verb** which is called **declarative** structure.

stereotype
With reference to a fictional character in a story this would mean someone who is perceived not as an individual but as representative of a fixed type.

story
A told or written **narrative**. This **genre** is very varied, but usually stories are written chronologically with characters, dialogue, setting and a series of events that finally reach a conclusion. Stories are written to entertain and engage readers, and often to challenge them. Pupils from the earliest years in school and throughout their formal education are required in the English

National Curriculum to read a wide range of stories and to write them.

Dorling Kindersley's 3–7 CD ROMs on a range of stories (e.g. Rainbow Fish, Little Polar Bear) include a range of activities for reading.

story board

A sequenced plan in pictures of the key moments in the plot of a story which can be used as an aid to **composition** or **comprehension**.

story plan

A list of headings, notes or a diagram that is created before writing in order to give a structure.

story starter

A stimulus for **composition**, sometimes written on card for pupils to use as a writing resource, e.g.

'I've been waiting for you,' whispered a soft and unfamiliar voice . . .
On and on we continued, though the mist was closing in . . .
You may remember how it all began . . .

story structure

The framework underpinning a story, conventionally analysed as beginning, middle and end.

stress

The force with which an utterance is articulated. Some parts of words or sentences are spoken with more force than others and so sound louder and more emphasised. In English the position of stress may vary from word to word, e.g. *consonant, computer, contravene.* Stress may differentiate one word from another, e.g. *transport* (noun)/*transport* (verb).

structure

In **grammar** a meaningful pattern of language within a unit is known as a grammatical structure. Structure is an ordered arrangement of elements. In the **clause** the elements of structure would be subject, verb, object, complement, adverbial, e.g. *My brother calls me a nuisance, sometimes.*

subheading

An organisational device usually found in non-fiction texts signalling a chunk of written material that is a category of the main text. It often makes use of bold type or underlining.

subject

An element of **clause** structure that is closely linked with the verb. In statements, the subject comes before the verb, e.g. *I am thinking.* In questions, the subject follows the first verb e.g. *Am I thinking?* The subject may be the agent in the sentence, e.g. *He visited the doctor.*

subjunctive mood

In English the form of the verb used to express wishes and hypothetical meanings, e.g. God <u>save</u> the queen; If I <u>were</u> you . . .

subordinate clause

A dependent clause which is embedded in a sentence, either before or after the **main clause**. It does not have independent status, e.g. *The champion, <u>who had fallen in practice</u>, now gave a faultless performance in the men's final.* A subordinate clause gives additional information on something in the main clause.

subordinating conjunction

A type of conjunction that signals a **subordinate clause**, e.g. *until, as long as, if . . . then.*

substitution

Replacement of a longer construction with a **pro-form** in order to shorten a sentence or avoid repetition, e.g. *He ran all the way home and I did as well.* The word 'did' is the pro-form substitute for 'ran all the way home'.

subtext

A message that is implicit and not stated in words, which a sophisticated reader could infer from what is actually presented.

suffix

A **morpheme** added to the end of a whole word which can be inflectional or derivational. An inflectional suffix changes the tense of a word, e.g. *skate/skated* (present to past) or alters its grammatical status, e.g. *dog/dogs* (singular to plural). A derivational suffix alters the word class e.g. *faith/faithful* (noun to adjective).

summarise

To condense a text or part of it orally or in writing by picking out its main points after close reading and comprehension. See **reorganisation**.

superlative

A form of **adjective** which involves comparing to the highest degree and made by adding 'est' to the base form, e.g. *tallest*. An alternative is to put 'most' before the base form e.g. *most beautiful*. Irregular superlatives exist, such as *good/better/<u>best</u>* and *bad/worse/<u>worst</u>*. See **comparative**.

superordinate

A category in **semantics** referring to a word that lies 'above' a related word on a scale and is inclusive of this word, e.g. <u>*flower*</u>/*daisy, buttercup, bluebell*. The 'lower' terms are called **hyponyms**.

supported composition

A stage in **shared writing** where the focus is on pupils' composition, usually of a limited amount of text, and created individually or with a partner.

suspense

A **narrative** technique that involves delaying the moment when the readers' expectations are fulfilled.

syllable

A unit in **phonology** above phoneme, comprising a vowel with one or more consonants before or after it. Each syllable in a word is perceived as a beat. A word with one beat is known as monosyllabic, e.g. *book*. Words with more than one beat are known as polysyllabic, e.g. *professional* (four syllables).

Some world languages are based on a syllabic writing system where one sign represents one syllable, e.g. *cuneiform* – ancient Persian writing on clay tablets; further examples are *Katakana* and *Hiragana* used in modern Japan where the majority of the written symbols stand for a consonant followed by a vowel phoneme.

synonym

A word having a similar meaning to another, e.g. *dry/arid*. Generally, synonyms are not completely interchangeable, for each word has its own subtle shade of meaning.

synopsis

A written summary.

syntactic cue

A strategy for reading and interpreting a text that uses grammatical features as aids to understanding.

syntax

The structure of the sentence and how the component parts are related. This is another term for grammar.

synthetic phonics

A way of teaching phonics in a carefully structured sequence. The method relies on teaching one-to-one matching between letters and **phonemes**. Pupils sound each phoneme and blend them into whole words. See **analytic phonics**.

system

A system in grammar consists of a set or finite number of items amongst which a choice must be made, e.g. *the number system in English with its singular/ plural choice*.

table
A list arranged in columns.

tabulation grid
A matrix used to help readers record information they have researched in a structured way so that the notes may be used as a basis for further writing.

tag question
An **interrogative** structure placed at the end of a statement, e.g. *You will be on time, won't you? They're not at home, are they?* A casual tag might be used in speech e.g. *You will phone, OK?*

tailpiece
An ornamental design at the end of a chapter in a book.

talk log
A written evaluation produced by a pupil about his or her contribution to speaking and listening activities.

talk for writing
Discussion that precedes and supports writing. In talking pupils think about the intended text, its content, structure and purpose. They may practise telling and retelling through the use of puppets or role play and thereby generate appropriate vocabulary. Oral rehearsal of what is going to be written helps pupils to write coherently. (See the National Literacy Strategy document *Developing Early Writing*, DfEE, 2001, p. 15.)

talk partner
Someone who shares a conversation with you and may help clarify your thoughts. See **response partner.**

tanka
A poetic form having five lines and a syllable pattern of 575 (as in haiku) then two extra lines with seven syllables in each, e.g.

> *an icicle clings*
> *tenaciously to the eaves*
> *its small glassy spike*
> *beginning to shrink and weep*
> *in the wintry sun*

tautology
The unnecessary repetition of an idea in different words, e.g. *He repainted his house again.*

teacher talk
The speech structures used by teachers for specific purposes in classroom teaching.

teacher in role

A **drama strategy** in which the teacher plays the part of a character in the drama. Pupils may also be working in role.

teaching at the point of writing

1. A teaching strategy in which the emphasis is on teaching and **modelling** writing **composition** or **transcriptional** elements to the whole class on the board before the pupils attempt it themselves. In the demonstration the teacher speaks aloud his/her thought processes which contribute to the composition and the transcribing of it. After teacher **demonstration** or modelling, the pupils may be involved in **supported composition**, in which they attempt small sections of writing independently or in pairs, informed by the teacher's previous demonstration of it. Small white boards may be used by individuals or pairs at this stage. This is an approach advocated in the DfEE *Grammar for Writing and Developing Early Writing* documents. It contrasts with previous approaches to the teaching of writing in which pupils 'had a go' themselves, making possible errors. The piece of writing would be improved in subsequent drafts.

2. A strategy which focuses on supporting pupils in making decisions about their writing at the time of composition rather than giving help in the form of correction after the writing has been produced. See **intervention.**

The National Literacy Strategy document Grammar for Writing (DfEE, 1999, p.12) offers information and support.

tense

Present or **past** time indicated in grammar by the verb. Present tense uses the base verb which changes in the third person singular, e.g. *I remember, she remembers.* Past tense adds 'ed' to the base verb, e.g. *they remembered.* Some verbs have irregular past tense forms, e.g. *see/saw.* There is no separate future tense form in English and future time is expressed in a number of ways, e.g. *She will arrive soon. She arrives soon. She is going to arrive soon.*

terminology

A set of words or terms used in a particular context, e.g. grammatical terminology.

text

A piece of writing produced according to the conventions of the genre.

text level

National Literacy Strategy term for work relating to comprehension, composition, reading strategies and structure of textual genres.

text type
A classification of texts which share common language and structural features, which reflect similarity of purpose. An alternative term is **genre.**

textual feature
An attribute of a text which is particular to a **genre**, usually an aspect of vocabulary or structure, e.g. *time-related connectives in instruction texts.*

theme
1.   The subject of a piece of writing.
2.   The first part of a sentence, which assumes prominence because of its position.

thesaurus
A reference book that groups words of similar meaning together and enables the reader to find **synonyms**.

thought tracking
A **drama strategy** by which characters' thoughts and ideas may be made public by speaking aloud.

time line
A line marked to show a sequence of events or time scale.

time out
1.   A brief time provided during a class activity for individuals or pairs to talk and think.

2.   A moment during **forum theatre** when the actors ask advice from the group or when members change roles.

3.   A 'cooling down' time when teachers remove a pupil from a particular context to reduce the occurrence of certain behaviours.

time scale
The period of time over which the events in a story or text take place.

time slip
An interruption in the **chronology** of a story which involves a move to a different point in time, e.g. *Children of Winter by Berlie Doherty.*

title page
The page inside a book's front cover displaying the title, author and illustrator.

tone group
A unit in **phonology** which carries meaningful patterns of **pitch**, e.g. *a rising pitch often conveys a question.*

tongue twister

A phrase or sentence to practise enunciation skills, but which is tricky to say because of repetitive sound patterns, e.g. *An amazing American amassing a million anemones a month.*

top-down

A description of a way to process information that relies on a reader's knowledge, expectation and prediction skills. This contrasts with a **bottom-up** approach.

traditional tale

A short story which has been told or written through many generations in a particular culture, e.g. *Goldilocks, Jack and the Beanstalk.* See **genre**.

transitive

Followed by an **object**. Transitive **verbs**, e.g. *bring, need, get*, need an object to complete them, e.g. *My friend will bring her bike.*

transcription skills

Skills involved in writing things down, such as spelling and handwriting.

trigraph

A group of three letters that represent one **phoneme**, e.g. *bri<u>dge</u>.*

trilogy

A sequence of three books with certain aspects in common, e.g. *Friends and Foes by A. Turnbull.*

typeface

A printed form of a writing system which is an important element of design.

typography

The design of a whole book including features such as size and shape, typeface, spacing. Typography may be used creatively by writers, e.g. *e. e. cummings, the poet.*

underline

To draw a line under a word or words often for emphasis. Titles or headings in particular may be underlined.

unvoiced

Without vibration of the vocal chords. Some **consonants** show a contrast between unvoiced and **voiced** pairs e.g. /f/ is unvoiced as in *fat*; v is voiced as in *vat*; /th/ is unvoiced as in *thin*; /th/ voiced as in *this*; /p/ is unvoiced as in *pin* and /b/ is voiced as in *bin*.

unit

A category of grammar referring to a stretch of language that carries a meaningful pattern. The following units, sentences, carry the same pattern of clauses: subordinate followed by main clause. *If you do that, you will be sorry. When Jane left, the party was nearly over.* Units work in hierarchies with larger units made up of smaller ones, e.g. sentences are made up of smaller units called clauses.

upper case

The capitalised form of letters.

verb

One of the grammatical **word classes** comprising words that express an action e.g. *jump*, a state of being, e.g. *seem*, or thinking, e.g. *consider*. The verb plays a vital role in the structure of the clause.

verb phrase

A group of words making up the verb element, e.g. *are playing, did leave, have been talking.*

verbal rehearsal

A strategy involving pupils or teachers speaking aloud a sentence or short text so that they can hear how it sounds and think about vocabulary and grammatical structure and if it fulfils their intentions. It is a strategy recommended in the National Literacy Strategy document *Developing Early Writing* (DfEE, 2001). See **talk for writing.**

viewpoint

1. The position of the viewer in relation to a picture.

2. The personal perspective from which a story is told.

vignette

1. A small ornamental design used to decorate a section of text.
2. A scenario representing a problem for which teachers or pupils may suggest possible resolutions.

visual cue

A source of information, such as a picture, which readers may use to help them decode and interpret a text.

visualisation

A teaching strategy where a pupil closes his or her eyes and imagines the details of a scene, sometimes guided by the voice of a teacher. This can be used to support pupils in clarifying their ideas for a piece of writing. It is also used as a drama technique.

visual literacy
The ability to interpret images and gain meaning from media other than writing.

vocabulary
The words of a language.

voice

1. The difference between **active** and **passive** forms of the **verb**.

2. The character from whose perspective a story or text is written.

voiced
With vibration of the vocal chords. In English some **consonant** pairs show a contrast between voiced and **unvoiced** sounds, e.g. voiced /b/ in bit and unvoiced /p/ in pit.

vowel
1. A **voiced** sound made with no obstruction to the airflow, e.g. /a/, /e/, /i/, /o/, /u/ and the neutral vowel, schwa.

2. The letters a, e, i, o, u in the alphabet.

vowel phoneme
A vowel sound represented by one or more letters, e.g. s*ee*n, afr*ai*d, w*ou*ld, ch*a*t.

In the *National Literacy Strategy Progression in Phonics* (DfEE, 2000a) the following are the 20 vowel phonemes which are taught to pupils: /a/, /e/, /i/, /o/, /u/, /ae/, /ee/, /ie/ /oe/ /ue/, /oo/, /ar/, /ur/, /or/, /au/, /er/, /ow/, /oi/, /air/, /ear/.

Vowel phonemes	Examples
/a/	l*a*p
/ae/	p*ai*n, cr*a*ne, p*ay*, t*a*ble, str*aigh*t
/air/	f*air*, c*are*, w*ear*, th*eir*
/ar/	f*ar*, l*a*st, h*ear*t
/au/	r*aw*, b*a*ll, *au*thor, w*ar*n
/e/	l*e*t, h*ea*d
/ee/	w*ee*d, m*ea*t, compl*e*te, ch*ie*f, med*ia*
/ear/	n*ear*, h*ere*, ch*eer*, t*ier*
/ew/	n*ew*, d*ue*
/i/	p*i*n, w*o*men, *E*nglish, s*y*stem
/ie/	m*y*, m*i*ne, wr*i*ting, h*igh*, cr*ie*d,
/o/	p*o*t, w*a*tch
/oo/	l*oo*k, p*u*sh, c*oul*d
/oo/	br*oo*m, tw*o*, thr*ough*
/oe/	m*ow*, r*o*pe, m*oul*d, c*oa*t, b*o*ld

/oi/	toy, foil
/or/	for, door, more
/ow/	now, bough, about
/u/	fun, cover
/ur/	fur, fir, her, word, search
/ue/	flue, flew, flu, rule

schwa apostrophe, sharpen, pencil, bottom, circus, collar, winter, author, figure, progression

wait time

A strategy to develop participation in discussion. The teacher asks an open-ended question and does not require a response until after a period of thinking time has elapsed.

wh-words

Question words, e.g. *when, where, why, who, how.*

whole word

An approach to reading that relies on visual recognition and memorising of a complete word rather than decoding by **segmenting** phonically.

Whole word recognition is a strategy highlighted in the Nartional Literacy Strategy **searchlights** model. Lists of **high frequency** and **medium frequency** words are provided in the National Literacy Strategy for pupils to learn in each year of primary schooling.

An alternative term is **sight word.**

word

A spoken or written sign that in the hierarchy of grammar is found above morpheme. It is formed from letters or sounds and carries meaning. Words are grouped together to create phrases.

word class

A grouping of members of a unit in terms of their function. The main word classes are **verb, noun, adjective, adverb, pronoun, determiner, preposition** and **conjunction**. 'Parts of speech' is an older term.

word level

National Literacy Strategy term for work relating to phonics, sight words, spelling and handwriting

Words at Work (Phenix, various) are useful word and sentence level workbooks.

writing

The requirements for the teaching of writing at Key Stages 1 and 2 are laid out in the National Curriculum Programmes of Study for writing (En3), which specify the knowledge, skills, understanding and breadth of study.

Writing Guides from Scholastic are photocopiable activities for different primary age-groups for writing a range of fiction genres: fantasy, humorous, scary stories, sci-fi, adventure, instructions, and fairy stories.

writing analysis

1. An assessment procedure or **miscue** process to evaluate the strengths and weaknesses in a piece of writing.

2. Deconstruction of a text to make the structure explicit or to investigate a writer's individual style.

writing frame

An aid to composition that provides aspects of the structural form and vocabulary of a particular genre to create a framework that supports writing. The written frameword is usually provided on a worksheet for children to complete. An example would be time (*temporal) connectives provided for the sequenced steps needed to achieve the goal in an instructional text: First . . . Next . . . Then . . . After that . . . Finally . . .* The amount of help given, a form of **scaffolding** of learning, may vary with individual needs, though the aim is always the same: independent writing from pupils who have internalised the generic structures.

writing alongside role

Writing produced after a drama experience from the viewpoint of a particular character.

Just Write and Write Away is a set of videos providing contexts for writing for a range of ages from Channel Four TV.

writing in role

Writing during the action of a drama. This involves adopting the perspective of a fictional character to create a written text that is authentic and requires its own specific audience.

National Literacy Strategy range of texts to be taught

Non-fiction text types (genres)

- **Autobiographies and biographies**, diaries, journals, letters, anecdotes, records of observations which recount experiences or events (Y6T1)

- **Simple non-fiction texts** (YR)

- **Signs, labels, captions, lists, instructions** (Y1T1)

- **Recounts:**
  Recounts (YR); Recounts of observations, visits, events (Y1T3)
  Recounts of events, activities, visits, observational records, news reports (Y5T1)

- **Information texts:**
  Information texts (Y1T2, 3; Y2T3)
  Information texts on topics of interest (Y3T1)
  Information texts on same or similar themes (Y4T2)
  Information texts linked to other curricular areas (Y4T3)

- **Reports:**
  Non-chronological reports (Y1T2; Y2T3; Y3T1; Y5T2; Y6T1)
  Non-chronological reports linked to work from other subjects (Y6T3)
  Reports and articles in newspapers and magazines (Y4T1)

- **Explanations** (Y2T2; Y4T2)

- **Processes, systems, operations, using context from other subjects** (Y5T2; Y6T3)

- **Instructions:**
  Instructions (Y2T1; Y3T2; Y4T1)
  Instructional texts: rules, recipes, directions, instructions, showing how things are done (Y5T1)

- **Letters:**
  Letters written for a range of purposes, e.g. to recount, explain, enquire, congratulate, complain (Y3T3)

- **Persuasive writing:**
  Persuasive writing: adverts, flyers, circulars (Y4T3)
  Putting or arguing a point of view, letters, commentaries, leaflets to persuade, criticise, protest, support, object, complain (Y5T3)

- **Discussion texts**: debates, editorials (Y4T3; Y6T2)

- **Journalistic writing** (Y6T1)

- **Formal writing**: notices, public information documents (Y6T2)

Alphabetically ordered texts and reference texts

- **Dictionaries:**
  Simple dictionaries (Y1T2)
  Dictionaries (Y2T2; Y3T1; Y5T3)
  Dictionaries without illustrations (Y3T2; Y6T3)

- **Glossaries** (Y2T2)

- **Indexes** (Y2T2; Y3T3)

- **Thesauruses** (Y3T1; Y3T2; Y5T3; Y6T3)

- **Directories** (Y3T3)

- **Encyclopaedias** (Y3T3)

- **IT sources** (Y5T3; Y6T3)

Stories

- **Traditional stories** (YR; Y2T2; Y3T2)

- **Stories with patterned language** (YR; Y2T2)

- **Stories with predictable structures and patterns** (YR; Y1T1, 2; Y2T2)

- **Stories with familiar settings** (Y1T1; Y2T1; Y3T1)

- **Fairy stories** (Y1T2)

- **Stories from a range of cultures** (Y1T2; Y2T2; Y4T3)

- **Plays** (Y1T2)

- **Stories about fantasy worlds** (Y1T3)

- **Extended stories** (Y2T3)

- **Stories by significant children's authors** (Y2T3; Y5T1)

- **Novels by significant children's authors** (Y5T1)

- **Different stories by the same author** (Y2T3; Y3T3; Y4T3)

- **Humorous stories** (Y2T3)

- **Stories with related themes** (Y3T2)

- **Adventure and mystery stories** (Y3T3)

- **Historical stories** (Y4T1)

- **Short novels** (Y4T1)

- **Playscripts** (Y4T1; Y5T1)

- **Stories/novels about imagined worlds: sci-fi, fantasy adventures** (Y4T2)

- **Stories in series** (Y4T2)

- Stories/short novels that raise issues: bullying, bereavement, injustice (Y4T3)
- Traditional stories from a range of cultures (Y5T2)
- Novels and stories from a variety of cultures and traditions (Y5T3)
- Classic fiction and drama by long established authors: e.g. Shakespeare plays (Y6T1)
- Adaptations of classics on film and TV (Y6T1)
- Longer established stories and novels from more than one genre : mystery, humour, sci-fi, historical, fantasy worlds (Y6T2)
- Comparison of work by significant children's authors (different authors' treatment of same theme; same author) (Y6T3)

Fiction texts
- **Myths** (Y3T2)
- **Legends** (Y3T2)
- **Fables** (Y3T2)
- **Parables** (Y3T2)
- **Myths, legends, fables from a range of cultures** (Y5T2)

Poetry
- **Traditional, nursery and modern rhymes, chants, action verses, poetry** (YR; Y1T2)
- **Rhymes** with predictable and repetitive patterns (YR; Y1T1)
- **Poems** with familiar, predictable and patterned language from a range of cultures (Y1T2)
- **Poems** with patterned and predictable structures (Y1T3)
- **Poems** on similar themes (Y1T3)
- **Poems** with familiar settings (Y2T1)
- **Poems** from other cultures (Y2T2; Y5T3)
- **Poems** with predictable and patterned language (Y2T2)
- **Poems** by significant children's poets (Y2T2; Y5T1)
- **Texts with language play**: riddles, tongue twisters, humorous verse (Y2T3)
- **Poetry that plays with language**: word puzzles, puns, riddles (Y3T3)
- **Humorous poetry** (Y3T3)
- **Poems** based on common themes: space, school, animals, families, feelings, viewpoints. (Y4T1)

- **Poems** based on observation and the senses (Y3T1)
- **Shape poems** (Y3T1)
- **Oral and performance poetry from different cultures** (Y3T2; Y5T3)
- **Classic and modern poetry** (Y4T2)
- **Classic and modern poetry from different cultures and times** (Y4T2)
- **Poetry in different forms:** haiku, cinquain, couplets, lists, thin poems, alphabets, conversations, monologues, syllabics, prayers, epitaphs, songs, rhyming forms, free verse. (Y4T3)
- **Concrete poetry** (Y5T1)
- **Longer classic poetry** (Y5T2)
- **Narrative poetry** (Y5T2)
- **Choral poetry** (Y5T3)
- **Classic poetry by long established authors** (Y6T1)
- **Range of poetic forms** (kennings, limericks, riddles, cinquain, tanka, poems written in other forms as adverts, letters, diary entries, conversations, free verse, nonsense verse) (Y6T2)
- **Comparison of work by significant children's poets (same author; different authors' treatment of same theme)** (Y6T3)

Features of fiction texts

Stories

Definition/purpose	Language features	Form/structure
• A told or written narrative. • This genre is very varied, but usually stories are written chronologically with characters, dialogue, setting and a series of events that finally reach a conclusion. • Stories are written to entertain and engage readers, and often to challenge them. • Pupils from the earliest years in school and throughout their formal education are required in the English National Curriculum to read a wide range of stories and to write them.	• Narrative text. • Dialogue.	• Written chronologically. • The scene is set and characters are introduced. A series of events takes place, moving towards a climax and finally being resolved.
	Characterisation	**Settings**
	• Fictional 'made-up' characters. • Characters are people who act in real-life ways that the reader can understand or empathise with.	• Generally set in places which represent reality.

Adventure stories

Definition/purpose	Language features	Form/structure
• An entertaining text which allows escape from reality. It is structured chronologically with a series of action-packed events which provide excitement and tension for the reader, e.g. *Agent Z Stories* by M. Haddon. • Often sets out to solve a problem, conduct a rescue or prevent a disaster from happening. • Journeys are often involved, sometimes ranging over different countries. • May have a fantasy element, but usually realistic settings and characters. • Often good versus bad.	• Usually past tense. • Narrative text. • Short sentences increase pace. • Told in the first or third person. • Use of connectives and cohesive devices to tie the story together. • Descriptive words: adjectives, adverbs and verbs used to create an impact. • Dialogue.	• Place, characters and time described in the opening. • A chronological series of action-packed, cliff-hanging events to build suspense, culminating in a denouement. • Fast-moving plot. • Progress and set-backs occur. • Time shifts or flashbacks may be used. • The narrator may be absent or one of the characters.
	Characterisation	**Settings**
	• Humans or animals, sometimes stereotypical. • Good and bad characters. • One particular character may be in danger. • A heroine/hero often emerges as the problem is resolved. • Familiar characters who become heroes and heroines. • In series same characters are often used.	• May take place in the past, present or future. • Often set in other lands, or dangerous locations. • Descriptions of settings add to tension, apprehension or fear. • Sometimes stereotypical settings.

Fairy tales/folk tales/traditional tales

Definition/purpose	Langue features	Form/structure
• Children's stories which have an oral tradition and several different versions. • Characters are archetypal. • They are usually set in the past and use recognisable devices such as challenges, magic numbers and patterns of language. Magical numbers 3 or 7 often feature; sometimes this is termed the 'rule of three' and is evident in The Three Bears, The Three Little Pigs, The Three Billy Goats Gruff, 'three wishes', etc. • They often have a fantasy element. • Plots are often formulaic and predictable. Themes may include conflict between good and evil, e.g. *Beauty and the Beast, Sleeping Beauty.* • Traditional tales are short stories which have been told or written through many generations in a particular culture, e.g. *Jack and the Beanstalk.* • To entertain. • They often have a moral element.	• Narrative text. • Some dialogue. • Repeated phrases (The wolf in The Three Little Pigs repeatedly threatens: 'I'll huff and I'll puff and I'll blow your house down').	• Begins with formulaic starters such as 'Long, long ago....' or 'Once upon a time there lived....' • The scene is set where a character is revealed to be in danger. • A number of events occur, sometimes patterned or repeated, often threatening the main character. • The main character happily survives and the story culminates with a generally happy resolution. • Often a happy ending.
	Characterisation	**Settings**
	• Predictable stereotypical characters. • Humans or animals with human characteristics. • Sometimes extraordinary invented characters. • Traditionally there are good characters and wicked characters. • Traditional characters and roles side by side with fantasy characters who perform magical acts. • Normal lives often interrupted by supernatural beings (such as the fairy godmother in Cinderella) or events (a carriage appears to take Cinderella to the ball). • Characters with social status who have lives removed from normality (princesses, queens, emperors, princes) often come into contact with characters who live 'normal' lives. The differences between their experiences is often emphasised. • Objects are sometimes given the attributes of people.	• Set in past times (Long, long ago...) or partially imaginary worlds (In a far-off land...). • Often traditional recognisable settings with additional fantasy features. • Often involves woods, houses or palaces. • Sometimes a world governed by laws which are not traditional ones.

Myths

Definition/purpose	Language features	Form/structure
• Stories about heroes and their dealings with gods, fabulous creatures and monsters. There are human truths to be learned from these tales as well as understanding about the natural world and its creation e.g. *Wanderings of Odysseus by R. Sutcliff.* • Often stories which have been passed down through generations in an oral tradition.	• Narrative text. • Past tense.	• A series of events culminating in an ending which may not be a happy one. Good does not always triumph over evil.
	Characterisation	**Settings**
	• Often featuring gods and imaginary, mythical creatures or people.	• Set in different imaginary worlds where normal features of life are altered, a world governed by laws albeit not traditional ones.

Legends

Definition	Language features	Form/structure
• A heroic story set in the past. • There may be underlying truth if based on a real-life character e.g. *Arthur High King of Britain by Michael Morpurgo.* • Recognisable features of daily life plus fantasy elements. • Often stories which have been passed down through generations in an oral tradition. • Often has moral elements.	• Narrative text.	• A series of events culminating in an ending which may or may not be happy.
	Characterisation	**Settings**
	• Often featuring heroic fictional characters.	• A world governed by laws although sometimes not conventional ones. • Set in the distant past.

Fables

Definition	Language features	Form/structure
• A moral tale in prose or poetry that sometimes uses animals to reveal human weaknesses. Jean de la Fontaine and Aesop are renowned fable writers of the past. Tony Ross and Vivian French have produced contemporary versions of some of their tales. • Recognisable features of daily life plus fantasy elements.		• Begins with characters and setting followed by a series of events culminating in a lesson learned. • Concludes with the moral of the tale (1984) *What is the Truth* — a farmyard fable for the young. *Ted Hughes* Faber & Faber, London
	Characterisation	**Settings**
	• Humans and animals with human characteristics.	• Often set in the past.

Parables

Definition/purpose	Language features	Form/structure
• A story whose purpose is to teach or explain a moral or religious issue, often using metaphors often referring to stories in the bible. • Parables may be written in prose or verse e.g. *The Parable of the Old Men and the Young* by *Wilfred Owen.*	• Narrative.	• Story format.
	Characterisation	**Settings**
	• Characters are humans; often biblical characters.	• Often biblical.

Scary stories

Definition/purpose	Language features	Form/structure
• A genre of children's books in which the subject content is frightening e.g. *Chills run down my Spine by J. Vivelo, Creepies (series) by Rose Impey.* • The reader's fears and feelings are exploited.	• Narrative text. • Short sentences to build tension. • Rhetorical questions used. • Descriptions of sounds. • Dialogue. • Usually past tense. • Descriptive. adjectives, adverbs, verbs.	• Story structure. • Begins with characters and settings followed by a series of events, building suspense to a frightening climax before culminating in a resolution.
	Characterisation	**Settings**
	• Children and adults. • Good and evil characters. • Emphasis on characters feelings and senses.	• Traditionally frightening places such as graveyards, ruins, empty houses. Often at night. • A scary atmosphere is built through sensory description.

Science fiction

Definition/purpose	Language features	Form/structure
• A genre in which imagined but possible worlds and their inhabitants figure prominently. Children's writers include Terry Pratchett, Robert Swindells and Julia Jarman. • Often action packed and involving a fight against evil. • To entertain and stretch the imagination. • The reader has a virtual experience.	• Narrative text. • Dialogue.	• Story structure beginning with characters and setting followed by a series of incredible events where characters battle against challenges. • Culminates in a resolution.
	Characterisation	**Settings**
	• Often extraordinary invented characters, robots and aliens, recognisable as beings but with non-human or exaggerated features. • Characters live in a future time or another world. • Good and evil characters.	• Future time, outer space, other galaxies or other imaginary worlds. • Sometimes a familiar world with changed elements. • Often involves travel across time. • Use of science and technology.

Fantasy

Definition/purpose	Language features	Form/structure
• A fiction genre that aims to entertain and provide an exciting escape from reality. Its main ingredients are an imaginative plot, unusual characters and an element of magic. Writers of fantasy include Terry Pratchett, Susan Cooper, Lynne Reid Banks, Helen Cresswell and Kaye Umansky. • To entertain and enthrall. • Fantasy objects with magic powers may be featured, such as the ring in *Lord of the Rings* by J. R. R. Tolkien.	• Characterised by a lot of vivid description to create a detailed picture and build suspense. • Narrative text. • Dialogue.	• The story often follows characters on a journey or a quest to find or claim something. • The characters have to overcome challenges or win battles with villains on the way.

	Characterisation	Settings
	• Extraordinary invented characters, recognisable as beings but with non-human or exaggerated features. • Heroes, villains, guides.	• Fantastic, imaginary settings with a familiar basis. • Sometimes characters move from the real world into a fantasy world, as in *Alice in Wonderland* by Lewis Carroll. The move may be 'triggered' by an event such as looking in the mirror in Alice's case. • Sometimes the whole story is set in a fantasy world, such as *The Hobbit* by J. R. R. Tolkien. • The fantasy world has social rules and routines.

Poetry

Definition/purpose	Language features	Form/structure
An oral or written genre that often makes use of figurative language, rhythm and rhyme patterns and has a familiar structure, e.g. *sonnet, haiku*. In poetry, words are selected carefully and the meaning is often highly condensed. Prose and poetry are sometimes considered as opposites, but they both lie along a continuum; prose can be poetic in the way it is written and poetry can be written with the sound of prose. From the earliest stage of education and throughout the primary years, poetry is a genre that pupils are required, in the English National Curriculum, to read and later to write.	• Simile • Metaphor • Alliteration • Rhyme • Rhythm • Concise expression	• Varied

Features of non-fiction texts

Term	Definition/purpose	Language features	Form/structure
Autobiography	A story of one's own life.	• Past tense. • Time connectives.	• Proceeds through a factual account of one's own life. • Lists significant events in the writer's own life in a way which interests the reader. • Finishes with the present day.
Biography	A story of someone else's life.	• Past tense. • Time connectives.	• Proceeds through a factual account of a person's life chronologically. • Lists significant events in a person's life in a way which appeals to a reader.
Discussion text	Presents the different viewpoints of an argument or issue and comes to a conclusion.	• Simple present tense e.g. *students prefer lectures to seminars. They feel that lectures are more effective in conveying information.* • Impersonal plural form is used. • Connectives such as *however, therefore, consequently* are used as the logical discussion progresses.	• The subject is discussed in a general way rather than referring to one specific example, e.g. *people feel that more police are needed on the streets.*
Explanation text	Gives the detail of how something works. Provides an answer to a question about something. Perhaps tells us why something happened.	• Simple present tense. • Uses time connectives and causal connectives, e.g. *because, as a result of.*	• Starts with general introductory statement. • Logically proceeds through an explanation of how something happens. • Logically ordered. • Finishes when the explanation is complete.
Description	Tells what something looks like or is like; tells how something happened.	• Present tense. • Descriptive language, e.g. adjectives. • In descriptions of events may use time connectives.	• Sets out significant aspects of the subject or event in a descriptive way. • Events may be chronologically ordered but a different principle may be used.

92

Term	Definition/purposes	Language features	Form/structure
Information text	Wray (Oxford Literacy Web) considers this a better term for non-fiction.	• Sometimes considered an alterantive term for non-fiction.	• Sometimes considered an alterantive term for non-fiction.
Instruction text	Tells the sequence of how to do something.	• Imperative tense used, e.g. *Unscrew the outer case.* • The instructions focus on the general readership rather than an individual or group.	• A title or aim, e.g. *How to wire a fuse.* • A list of the materials/resourcs needed. • Numbered steps, bullet points or letters (a, b, c) progressing through the procedure in chronological order until the aim is achieved. • May include diagrams or pictures, which may be labelled in terms of their parts.
Record	Provides a written account of events and perhaps personal responses to them.	• Past tense. • Connectives. • Written in the third and first person.	• Title. • May be chronologically ordered or logically sequenced. • Provides an account of an event.
Recount	Tells about a past experience or event/s.	• Written in the past tense, e.g. *we went, we saw.* • Written in chronological order of the events. • Connectives of time used, e.g. *First, then.* • Often tells the events from one person's or several people's viewpoint.	• Usually sets the scene at the beginning, e.g. *Last week we went to a farm . . .* • An event or series of events is then described in time sequence (chronological), e.g. *We saw some cows and sheep.* • Often a concluding statement is made at the end, e.g. *We thanked the farmer very much and caught the bus home.*

Term	Definition/purpose	Language features	Form/structure
Report	Sets out factual information in a systematic way. Non-chronological. Describes or classifies.	• The simple present tense is used, e.g. *Giraffes are animals; they live in Africa.*	• Starts with a general statement about the nature of the subject, e.g. *Elephants are animals.* • A description and related facts about the subject follows, e.g. *what the animals look like, their habitat and food.* • Descriptions are usually impersonal and general, rather than specific, e.g. *describing elephants in general, not one specific elephant.* • May then give some specific examples, e.g. *African elephants have . . .* • Does not need to be in chronological order.
Persuasive text	Offers an argument for a particular point of view.	• The simple present tense is used, e.g. *Exercise is good for you. It keeps your body healthy.* • Connectives and linking phrases can be used, e.g. *because, however, as a result of this.*	• An introductory statement may state the case or argument which is to be presented, e.g. *There are too many cars on the roads in Britain.* • A sequence of statements is presented in a logical order, setting out reasons and evidence for a particular viewpoint.

Useful resources

For ease of use and reference, we have divided our list of resources into:

- *teaching resources*: printed and electronic resources to support classroom activities;
- *government publications*: publications and resources from the DfES, DfEE and QCA offering information and support;
- *further reading*: accessible publications to support your professional development;
- *teaching using ICT*: publications to support your use of ICT in the classroom;
- *useful websites*;
- *software*: high-quality software to use with your primary classes.

Teaching resources

100 Literacy Hours (1999). Leamington Spa: Scholastic.

BBC (1998) *Grammar* (video). London: BBC.

Bindon, R. (1999) *Shared and Guided Reading and Writing*, Vol. 2. Oxford: Ginn Heinemann Professional Development (First Steps, NLS edition).

The Book Project (1999). Harlow: Longman.

Braund, H. and Gibbon, D. (2001) *Activities for Writing Fairy Stories*, Writing Guides. Leamington Spa: Scholastic.

Bromley, H. (2000) *Book-Based Reading Games*. London: Centre for Language in Primary Education.

Dewsbury, A. (1999) *Shared and Guided Reading and Writing*, Vol. 1. Oxford: Ginn Heinemann Professional Development (First Steps, NLS edition).

Discovery World (1999). Oxford: Heinemann.

Finger Spelling Alphabet poster (1997) London. BBC Educational.

Focus English (2000) Oxford. Reed Educational and Professional.

Frost, H. et al. (2000) *On Target English*. Harlow: Longman.

Garnett, J. (2000a) *Playing with Words: Sound Effect Poems*, Pelican Guided Reading and Writing. Harlow: Longman.

Garnett, J. (2000b) *Poems to Perform*, Pelican Guided Reading and Writing. Harlow: Longman.

Gawith, G. (1999) *Reading Alive!* London: A. & C. Black.

Grant, K. (2000) *Special Needs Literacy Resources for Group Time*. Leamington Spa: Scholastic.

Harrison, S. (2000) *Non-fiction Writing Frames for Infants*. Dunstable: Belair Publications.

Institute of Education, University of London (1998) *Book Bands for Guided Reading*. London: Reading Recovery National Network.

Jolly Phonics. Jolly Learning.

Junior Focus (2002) Leamington Spa: Scholastic.

Just Write and *Write Away* (videos) (2001). London. Channel Four TV.

Launch into Literacy. (2000) Oxford: Oxford University Press.

Learning Targets for Literacy (1999). Cheltenham: Stanley Thornes.

Literacy Land (2001). Harlow: Longman.

Lovatt, M. (2001) *Activities for Writing Fantasy Stories*, Writing Guides. Leamington Spa: Scholastic.

Matthews, G. and Howell, G. (2000) *Here's One I Wrote Earlier*. Exeter: Learning Matters.

Merchant, G. (2001) *Activities for Writing Sci-Fi Stories*, Writing Guides. Leamington Spa: Scholastic.

Morgan, M. (2001) *How to Teach Poetry Writing at Key Stage 2*. London: David Fulton.

Morgan, M. (2002) *How to Teach Poetry Writing at Key Stage 1*. London: David Fulton.

Opitz, M. F. (1998) *Good-bye Round Robin: Twenty-five Effective Oral Reading Strategies.* Portsmouth, NH: Heinemann.

Orme, D. et al. (2001) *Literacy Line-Up*. London: Evans Educational.

Palmer, S. and Morgan, M. (2000) *Big Book Grammar*. London: Heinemann.

Pelican Shared Writing: Fiction and Non Fiction Resource Books (2001) London: Pearson Educational.

Phenix, J. (various) (1999) *Words at Work*. Dunstable: Folens.

Phonicability (2000). Hopscotch.

Powell, J. (2002) *Activities for Writing Adventure Stories*, Writing Guides. Leamington Spa: Scholastic.

Puddick, J., (2001) *Word Games*. London: BBC Educational Publishing.

Read and Respond (2000). Leamington Spa: Scholastic.

Redfern, A. (1998) *Developing Literacy Skills*. Hopscotch.

Reeve (1998) *Spelling and Phonics*. Leamington Spa: Scholastic.

Riley, J. (1999) *Teaching Reading at Key Stage 1 and Before*, Stanley Thornes Teaching Primary English series. Cheltenham: Stanley Thornes.

Rhyme World. (1998) Oxford: Heinemann.

Soundstart. (1998) Cheltenham: Stanley Thornes.

Stanley Thornes Primary Literacy. (2000) Cheltenham: Stanley Thornes.

Thomas, H. (2001) *Activities for Writing Scary Stories*, Writing Guides. Leamington Spa: Scholastic.

Government publications and guidance

DfEE/QCA (1999) *National Curriculum Handbook for Primary Teachers in England*. London: DfEE.

DfEE (1998) *NLS Framework for Teaching from Reception to Year 6*. London: DfEE.

DfEE (1999) *NLS Grammar for Writing*, with CD Rom. London: DfEE.

DfEE (2000) *NLS Progression in Phonics—Materials for Whole-class Teaching*, with CD-ROM. London: DfEE.

DfEE (2001) *Developing Early Writing*, with CD Rom. London: DfEE.

DfES (2001) *Shared Writing on School Placement*. London. DfES.

DfES (2001) *ICT in the Literacy Hour: Whole-class Teaching*. London: DfES.

National Centre for Literacy and Numeracy (1999) *Spelling Bank: Lists of Words and Activities for the Key Stage 2 Spelling Objectives*. London: National Centre for Literacy and Numeracy.

QCA (1999) *Teaching Speaking and Listening at Key Stages 1 and 2*. London: QCA.

QCA/DfEE (2000) *Curriculum Guidance for the Foundation Stage*. London: DfEE/QCA.

Further reading

Andrews, R. (2003) *The Impact of ICT on Literacy Education*. London: Routledge Falmer.

Bage, G. (1999) *Narrative Matters: Teaching and Learning History Through Story*. London: Falmer Press.

Bain, R. (1998) *The Primary Grammar Book: Finding Patterns – Making Sense*. Sheffield: NATE.

Baldwin, P. and Fleming, K. (2002) *Play in the Text*. London: Routledge Falmer.

Barrs, M. and Cook, V. (2001) *The Reader in the Writer*. London: CLPE.

Barton, D., Hamilton, M. and Ivanic, R. (2000) *Situated Literacies*. London: Routledge.

Baxter, J. (2001) *Making Gender Work*. Reading: University of Reading.

Beard, R. (1998) *NLS Review of Research and Other Evidence*. London: National Literacy Strategy.

Bearne, E. and Watson, V. (2000) *Where Texts and Children Meet*. London: Routledge Falmer.

Bearne, E. (1998) *Making Progress in English*. London: Routledge Falmer.

Bearne, E. (ed.) (1998) *Use of Language across the Primary Curriculum*. London: Routledge.

Bearne, E. (2002) *Making Progress in Writing*. London: Routledge Falmer.

Bentley, D., Burman, C., Chamberlain, T., Clipson-Boyles, S., Gray, D., Holderness, J., Lynch, M. and Reid, D. (1999) *The Really Practical Guide to Primary English*. Cheltenham: Stanley Thornes.

Bibby, B. and Priest, S. (2000) *Sharing Poems*. Sheffield: NATE.

Bolton, G. (1998) *Acting in Classroom Drama*. Sheffield: Trentham Books.

Bolton LEA (1999) *The IT in Primary Literacy*.

Browne, A. (1996) *Developing Language and Literacy 3–8*. London: Paul Chapman Publishing.

Browne, A. (1998) *A Practical Guide to Teaching Reading in the Early Years*. London: Paul Chapman Publishing.

Browne, A. (1999) *Teaching Writing at KS1 and Before*. Cheltenham: Stanley Thornes.

Buzan, T. (1991) *Use Your Head*. London: BBC.

Cameron, D. (2000) *Good to Talk?* London: Sage Publications.

Campbell, R. (1993) *Miscue Analysis in the Classroom*. UKRA.

Carter, D. (2000) *Teaching Fiction in the Primary School: Classroom Approaches to Narratives*. London: David Fulton.

Carter, J. (1999) *Talking Books*. London: Routledge Falmer.

Carter, J. (2000) *Creative Writers: Developing Literacy Through Creative Writing*. London: Routledge Falmer.

Carter, J. (2000) *Rap It Up*. Birmingham: Questions.

Challen, D. (2001) *Primary English: Audit and Test*. Exeter: Learning Matters.

Cheminais, R. (2000) *Special Educational Needs for Newly Qualified and Student Teachers*. London: David Fulton.

Clay, M. (1979) *Concepts of Print: The Early Detection of Reading Difficulties,* 2nd edn. Auckland: Heinemann Education.

Clay, M. (1998) *By Different Paths to Common Outcomes.* York: Stenhouse Publishers.

Corbett, P. (2002) *How to Teach Fiction Writing at Key Stage 1.* London: David Fulton.

Corden, R. (2000) *Literacy and Learning Through Talk.* Oxford: Oxford University Press.

Crystal, D. (1996) *Rediscover Grammar.* Harlow: Longman.

Cullen, K. (ed.) (1999) *Chambers Guide to Effective Grammar.* Edinburgh: Chambers.

Cunningham, P. (2000) *Phonics They Use: Words for Reading and Writing.* New York: Longman.

Davison, J. and Moss, J. (1999) *Issues in English Teaching.* London: Routledge Falmer.

Dean, G. (2001) *Challenging the More Able Language User,* revised edn. NACE The National Association for able Children in Education: David Fulton.

Department for Education and Employment (1998) *The National Literacy Strategy.* London: DfEE.

Department for Education and Employment (2000) *The National Literacy Strategy: Grammar for Writing.* London: DfEE.

Department for Education and Employment (2001) *The National Literacy Strategy: Developing Early Writing.* London: DfEE.

Department for Education and Employment (1999) *The National Literacy Strategy Phonics: Progression in Phonics.* London: DfEE.

Dombey, H., and Mustafa, M. (1998) *Whole to Part Phonics: How Children Learn to Read and Spell.* London: Centre for Language in Primary Education.

Duncan, H. (2000) *Improving Literacy Skills for Children with Special Educational Needs.* London: Routledge Falmer.

Edwards, S. (1999) *Reading for All.* London: David Fulton.

Edwards, S. (1999) *Writing for All .* London: David Fulton.

Edwards, V. (1998) *The Power of Babel: Teaching and Learning in Multilingual Classrooms.* Stoke-on-Trent: Trentham Books.

Evans, J. (ed.) (2001) *The Writing Classroom: New Aspects of Writing and the Primary Child 3–11.* London: David Fulton.

Eve, J. (ed.) (1999) *Reading and Dyslexia: Visual and Attentional Processes.* London: Routledge.

Fisher, R. (2000) *First Poems for Thinking.* Oxford: Nash Pollock Publishing.

Fisher, R. (2001) *Inside the Literacy Hour: Learning from Classroom Experience.* London: Routledge Falmer.

Fisher, R., Lewis, M. and Brooks, G. (2002) *Raising Standards in Literacy.* London: Routledge Falmer.

Fountas, I. C. and Pinnel G. S. (1996) *Guided Reading: Good First Teaching for all Children.* Portsmouth, NH: Heinemann.

Frater, G. (2000) *Securing Boys' Literacy.* London: Basic Skills Agency.

Gamble, N. and Yates, S. (2002) *Exploring Children's Literature: Teaching the Language and Reading of Fiction.* London: Paul Chapman Publishing.

Garner, P. and Davis, J. (2001) *Introducing Special Educational Needs: A Companion Guide for Student Teachers*. London: David Fulton.

Glass, L. (2000) *Read! Read! Read! Training Effective Reading Partners*. Thousand Oaks, CA: Corwin Press.

Goatly, A. (2000) *Critical Reading and Writing: An Introductory Coursebook*. London: Routledge.

Goodwin, P. (2000) *Reading Aloud to Children*. Reading: Reading and Language Information Centre.

Goodwin, P. and Redfern, A. (1998) *Non-fiction in the Literacy Hour*. Reading: Reading and Language Information Centre.

Goodwin, P. (ed.) (2001) *The Articulate Classroom*. London: David Fulton.

Goodwin, P. (1999) *The Literacy Classroom*. Reading: Reading and Language Information Centre.

Graham, J. (1997) *Cracking Good Books*. Sheffield: NATE.

Graham, J. and Kelly, A. (2000) *Reading Under Control: Teaching Reading in the Primary School*, 2nd edn. London: David Fulton.

Graham, J. and Kelly, A. (1998) *Writing Under Control: Teaching Writing in the Primary School*. London: David Fulton.

Grainger, T. and Cremin, M. (2001) *Resourcing Classroom Drama 5–8*. Sheffield: NATE.

Grainger, T. and Cremin, M. (2001) *Resourcing Classroom Drama 8–14*. Sheffield: NATE.

Grant, K. (2000) *Supporting Literacy: A Guide for Classroom Assistants*. London: Routledge Falmer.

Gravelle, M. (2000) *Planning for Bilingual Learners: An Inclusive Curriculum*. Stoke-on-Trent: Trentham Books.

Gregory, E. (1996) *Making Sense of a New World*. London: Paul Chapman Publishing.

Grugeon, E. (1998) *Teaching Speaking and Listening in the Primary School*. London: David Fulton.

Guppy, P. (1999) *The Development of Independent Reading: Reading Support Explained*. Buckingham: Open University Press.

Hall, C. and Coles, M. (1999) *Children's Reading Choices*. London: Routledge.

Hall, J. (2002) *Creative Writing*. London: Routledge Falmer.

Hall, N. and Robinson, A. (1996) *Learning About Punctuation*. Clevedon: Multilingual Matters.

Hannon, P. (2000) *Reflecting on Literacy in Education*. London: Routledge Falmer.

Harrison, C. and Coles, M. (2001) *The Reading for Real Handbook*. London: Routledge Falmer.

Hiatt, K. and Rooke, J. (2002) *Creating and Writing Skills*. London: David Fulton.

Hobsbaum, A. (2002) *Guiding Reading: A Handbook for Teaching Guided Reading at Key Stage 2*. London: Institute of Education.

Hoodless, P. (1998) *History and English in the Primary School: Exploiting the Links*. London: Routledge.

Hunt, G. (2000) *Grammar and Punctuation: Pocket Guides to the Primary Curriculum*. Leamington Spa: Scholastic.

Johnson, J. (2001) *Passing the Literacy Skills Test.* Exeter: Learning Matters.

Jones, R. and Boys, R. (2002) *PGCE Professional Workbook Primary English.* Exeter: Learning Matters.

Leicester, M. (2002) *Stories for Assembly and the Classroom.* London: Routledge Falmer.

Lewis, D. (2001) *Reading Contemporary Picture Books.* London: Routledge Falmer.

Lewis, M. (1998) *Writing Across the Curriculum: Frames to Support Learning.* Reading: Reading and Language Information Centre.

Mackey, M. (2002) *Literacies across Media.* London: Routledge Falmer.

McWilliams, N. (1998) *What's in a Word? Vocabulary Development in Multilingual Classrooms.* Stoke-on-Trent: Trentham Books.

Mallett, M. (1999) *Young Researchers: Informational Reading and Writing in the Early and Primary Years.* London: Routledge Falmer.

Marsh, J. and Millard, E. (2000) *Literacy and Popular Culture.* London: Paul Chapman Publishing.

Martino, W. and Meyemm, B. (2001) *What about the Boys?* Buckingham: Open University Press.

Mason, M. (1998) *Grammar Dictionary.* Birmingham: Questions.

Matthews, G. and Howell, G. (2002) *Here's One I Wrote Earlier: Instant Resources for Shared and Modelled Writing.* Exeter: Learning Matters.

Maynard, T. (2001) *Boys and Literacy: Exploring the Issues.* London: Routledge Falmer.

Medwell, J. and Wray, D. (2002) *Using ICT in Primary English Teaching.* Exeter: Learning Matters.

Medwell, J., Wray, D., Minns, H., Griffiths, V. and Coates, E. (2002) *Primary English: Knowledge and Understanding.* Exeter: Learning Matters.

Medwell, J., Wray, D., Minns, H., Griffiths, V. and Coates, E. (2002) *Primary English: Teaching Theory and Practice.* Exeter: Learning Matters.

Merchant, G. and Thomas, H. (eds) *Non-Fiction for the Literacy Hour.* London (2001): David Fulton.

Millard, E. (1997) *Differently Literate: Boys, Girls and the Schooling of Literacy.* London: Falmer Press.

Moon, C. (2000) *Individualised Reading.* Reading: Reading and Language Information Centre.

NATE Drama Committee (2001) *Cracking Drama: Progression in Drama within English.* Sheffield: NATE.

Neill, H. (ed.) (2000) *Write Away: Primary.* London: TES.

Palmer, S. (2002) *How to Teach Writing Across the Curriculum at Key Stage 1.* London: David Fulton.

Pinker, S. (1994) *The Language Instinct.* Harmondsworth: Penguin.

Pollock, J. (1999) *English Grammar and Teaching Strategies: Lifeline to Literacy.* London : David Fulton.

Reid, D. and Bentley, D. (1996) *Read On! Developing Reading at Key Stage Two.* Leamington Spa: Scholastic.

Riley, J. (2000) *Developing Writing for Different Purposes: Teaching About Genre in the Early Years.* London: Paul Chapman Publishing.

Sassoon, R. (1995) *The Acquisition of a Second Writing System.* London: Intellect.

Sedgwick, F. (2000) *Writing to Learn*. London: Routledge Falmer.

Seeley, E. and Seeley, J. (1998) *All About English*. Oxford: Oxford University Press.

Stones, R. (ed.) (1999) *A Multicultural Guide to Children's Books 0–16*. Books for Keeps. Reading: Reading, Language Information Centre.

Styles, M. (1998) *From the Garden to the Street: Three Hundred Years of Poetry for Children*. London: Cassell.

Styles, M. and Arizpe, E. (2002) *Children Reading Pictures*. London: Routledge Falmer.

Tabor, D. (2002) *Young Writers at Transition*. London: Routledge Falmer.

Taylor, J., Freeman, M. and Bailey, J. (1998) *Ways with Plays*. Devon County Council.

Thomas, H. (1998) *Reading and Responding to Fiction: Classroom Strategies for Developing Literacy*. Leamington Spa: Scholastic.

Tyrrell, J. and Gill, N. (2000) *Coordinating English at KS1*. London: Routledge Falmer.

Tyrrell, J. (2001) *The Power of Fantasy in Early Learning*. London: Routledge Falmer.

Waters, M. and Martin, T. (1998) *Coordinating English at KS2*. London: Routledge Falmer.

Williams, J. D. and Dale, J. (1999) *The Teacher's Grammar Book*. Mahwah, N.J.: L. Erlbaum Associates.

Wilson, A. (2001) *Language Knowledge for Primary Teachers*. London: David Fulton.

Wilson, A. and Hughes, S. (eds) (1998) *The Poetry Book for Primary Schools*. London: The Poetry Society.

Wragg, E., Wragg, M., Haynes, G. and Chamberlin, R. (1998) *Improving Literacy in the Primary School*. London: Routledge Falmer.

Wray, D. and Lewis, M. (1997) *Extending Literacy*. London: Routledge Falmer.

Wray, D., Medwell, J., Poulson, L. and Fox, R. (2001) *Teaching Literacy Effectively in the Primary School*. London: Routledge Falmer.

Wyse, D. (1998) *Primary Writing*. Buckingham: Open University Press.

Wyse, D. and Jones, R. (2000) *Teaching English, Language and Literacy*. London: Routledge Falmer.

Teaching using ICT

BECTa (1998) *Primarily IT: Using IT to Support English, Maths and Science at KS2*. BECTa.

Bolton Curriculum ICT Centre (1998) *The IT in Primary Literacy*. Bolton Curriculum ICT Centre.

Bolton Curriculum ICT Centre (1998) *ICT for the Under Fives*. Bolton Curriculum ICT Centre.

Canterbury Christchurch College (1998) Talking about ICT in Subject Teaching.

Cook, D. and Findlayson, H. (1999) *Interactive Children, Communicative Teaching: ICT and Classroom Teaching*. Oxford: Oxford University Press.

De Cicco, E., Farmer, M. and Hargrave, C. (1999) *Activities for Using the Internet in Primary Schools*. London: Kogan Page.

Dick, R. (1998) *IT Starts Here*. Kettering: Castlefield Press.

Farmer, M. and Farmer, G. (2000) *Supporting Information and Communications Technology: A Handbook for Those Who Assist in Early Years Settings*. London: David Fulton.

Higgins, S. et al. (1999) *500 ICT Tips for Primary Teachers*. London: Kogan Page.

Lachs, V. (2000) *Making Multimedia in the Classroom: A Teachers' Guide*. Routledge Falmer.

Leask, M. (ed.) (2001) *Issues in Teaching using ICT*. Routledge Falmer

Leask, M. and Meadows, J. (ed.) (2000) *Teaching and Learning with ICT in the Primary School*. London: Routledge Falmer.

Loveless, A. and Ellis, V. (eds) (2001) *ICT, Pedagogy and the Curriculum*. London: Routledge Falmer.

McFarlane, A. (ed.) (1997) *Information Technology and Authentic Learning: Realising the Potential of Computers in the Primary School*. London: Routledge.

Monteith, M. (ed.) *IT for Learning Enhancement*. Exeter: Intellect Books.

Mosely, D. and Higgins, S. (1999) *Ways Forward with ICT: Effective Pedagogy Using ICT for Literacy and Numeracy in Primary Schools*. Newcastle: University of Newcastle.

Parker, B. and Yates, S. (2000) *Internet Matters: Making Sense of NGfL in Your Classroom*. TAG.

Poole, P. (ed.) (1998) *Talking About Information and Communications Technology in Subject Teaching: Primary*. Canterbury: Canterbury Christ Church College.

Sharp, J., Potter, J., Allen, J. and Loveless, A. (2000) *Primary ICT: Knowledge, Understanding and Practice*. Exeter: Learning Matters.

Shreeve, A. (ed.) (1997) *IT in English* series (*Planning and Management, Case Studies and Materials, Literature Review, Resources for Learning*). NCET.

Smith, H. (1999) *Opportunities for ICT in the Primary School*. Stoke-on-Trent: Trentham.

Somekh, B. and Davis, N. (eds) (1997) *Using Information Technology Effectively in Teaching and Learning*. London: Routledge.

Trend, R. et al. (1999) *Information and Communications Technology*. London: Letts Education.

Uppal, S. (2000) *ICT: Pocket Guides to the Primary Curriculum*. Leamington Spa: Scholastic.

Wegerif, R. and Scrimshaw, P. (1997) *Computers and Talk in the Primary Classroom*. Clevedon: Multilingual Matters.

Useful websites

BBC Education Online — www.bbc.co.uk/education/home/today/

BECTa — www.becta.org.uk/

DfES — www.dfes.gov.uk/index.shtml

National Grid for Learning — www.ngfl.gov.uk/index.html

Ofsted — www.ofsted.gov.uk/

PICTURE (Primary ICT Useful References/Reading/Resources)
   — www.ucsm.ac.uk/staff/dmurray/picture/

Primary Resources — www.primaryresources.co.uk/

QCA — www.qca.org.uk/

Roger Frost's Dataloggerama — www.rogerfrost.com/
Sites for Teachers — www.sitesforteachers.com/index.html
Teaching Ideas for Primary Teachers — www.teachingideas.co.uk/
Times Educational Supplement — www.tes.co.uk
TTA — www.teach-tta.gov.uk/
UK Schools Resources Page — www.liv.ac.uk/~evansjon/home.html
Virtual Teachers Centre — http://vtc.ngfl.gov.uk/

Software

A–Z (3–5 years). Inclusive Technology.
A–Zap (3–6 years). Tag.
Bailey's Book House (2–6 years). Iona.
Big ABC, Oxford Literacy Web. Sherston.
Clicker (4–11 years). Crick.
Early Literacy Skills (4–7years). Sunshine Multimedia.
Education City Online Schools Primary English (5–11 years). Cybermind.
The Email Detectives. Sherston.
First Keys to Literacy (4–8 years). Widgit.
First Words with Smudge (4–8 years). Storm.
The Grammar Show. Sherston.
I Love Spelling. Dorling Kindersley.
Lessonbank (teacher resource for a range of non-fiction texts). Belair.
Literacy Bank. Sherston.
Literacy Box. Sherston.
Little Monsters Literacy Pack (3–5 years) Ransom.
Making Sense with Letters (5–7 years). Inclusive Technology.
Making Tracks to Literacy (5–11 years). Widgit.
Matti Mole's Summer Holiday. Sherston.
Mr. Happy's Selection Box (3–7 years). Bradford Technology.
My Oxford Word Box (4–7 years). Oxford University Press.
Newstream Hotline (5–16 years). Actis.
Nursery Rhyme Time (4–6 years). Sherston.
OCR English Progress Tests (a range for 7–11 years). Folens.
Oxford Reading Tree Talking Stories. Sherston.
Percy's ABC (3–6 years). Neptune Computer.
Phontastic (4–7 years). AVP Computing.
The Punctuation Show. Sherston.
Reader Rabbit (3–8 years). The Learning Company.
Reading Zone. Sherston.
Rhyme and Analogy. Sherston.
Ridiculous Rhymes (4–6 years). Sherston.
The Sherston Naughty Stories. Sherston.
Sound Activities (4–6 years). Sherston.
Sound Activities, Oxford Literacy Web. Sherston.
Sound Stories, Oxford Literacy Web. Sherston.
Spelling Programme (5–6 years). Folens.
The Spelling Show. Sherston.
Spellmate. Sherston.
Startwrite. Sherston.

Talking Animated Alphabet (4–6 years). Sherston.
Talking Topics. Sherston.
Teacher's Cupboard. Sherston.
Teddy Bears' Picnic. Sherston.
Text Detectives. Sherston.
3–7. Dorling Kindersley.
Wordshark (5–14 years). White Space.
Worksheet Maker (teachers' resource to create worksheets for years 1–6).
      Open Mind.

Poems and books

This is a complete list of all poetry, story and reference book examples used within the text.

Poems

'Elegy on the Death of a Mad Dog' by Oliver Goldsmith, in *The Child's Garland*, ed. Coventry Patmore (Macmillan, 1862).

'Elegy Written in a Country Churchyard' by Thomas Gray, in *Poetry Please: One Hundred Popular Poems from the BBC Radio 4 Programme* (J. M. Dent, 1985).

'La Belle Dame Sans Merci' by John Keats, in *The New Oxford Book of English Verse*, ed. Helen Gardner (London, 1972).

The Lady of Shalott by Alfred, Lord Tennyson, illustrated by Charles Keeping (Oxford: Oxford University Press, 1986).

'The Parable of the Old Men and the Young' by Wilfred Owen, in *Voices* (the third book), ed. Geoffrey Summerfield (Penguin, 1968).

'The Pied Piper of Hamelin' by Robert Browning, in *The Oxford Book of Children's Verse*, eds I. and P. Opie (Oxford, 1973/93).

'Ode on the Death of a Favourite Cat Drowned in a Tub of Gold Fishes' by Thomas Gray, in *The New Oxford Book of English Verse*, ed. Helen Gardner (London, 1972).

'Ode to the North-East Wind' by Charles Kingsley, in *Poetry Please: One Hundred Popular Poems from the BBC Radio 4 Programme* (J. M. Dent, 1985).

Playtime Treasury, collection of oral poems by Pie Corbett (Kingfisher, 1989).

'The Rime of the Ancient Mariner' by Samuel Taylor Coleridge, in *The New Oxford Book of English Verse*, ed. Helen Gardner (London, 1972).

'The Sea' by James Reeves, in *Complete Poems for Children* (Heinemann, 1973).

'*Shall I compare thee to a summer's day*' by William Shakespeare. Classic Poems to Read Aloud selected by J. Berry. London: Kingfisher, 1997.

'The Star' by Jane Taylor, in *The Oxford Treasury of Children's Poems* by Michael Harrison and Christopher Stuart-Clark (Oxford: Oxford University Press, 1988).

The Upside-Down Frown, poems collected by Andrew Fusek Peters (Wayland, 1999).

Stories

Ahlberg, Janet and Ahlberg, Allan (1989) *Burglar Bill*. Mammoth.

Almond, David (1998) *Skellig*. Hodder.

Baker, Jeannie (1991) *Window*. Julia Macrae.

Barlow, Steve and Skidmore, Steve (1997) *The Lost Diary of Julius Caesar's Slave*. Collins.

Beck, Ian (2001) *Goldilocks and the Three Bears*. Oxford University Press.

Biro, V. (2000) *Jack and the Beanstalk*. Oxford University Press.

Branford, Henrietta (1997) *Fire, Bed and Bone*. Walker.

Browne, Anthony (1986) *A Walk in the Park*. Macmillan.
Burnett, Frances Hodgson (1999) *The Secret Garden*. Penguin.
Burningham, John (2001) *Mr. Grumpy's Outing*. Red Fox.
Carter, Angela (1991) *Sleeping Beauty and Other Favourite Fairy Tales* (of Charles Perrault, translated and retold by Angela Carter). Gollancz.
Coleman, Michael (1990s series) *The Internet Detectives*. Macmillan.
Crossley-Holland, Kevin (1985) *Storm*. Heinemann.
Dahl, Roald (1974) *Fantastic Mr. Fox*. Young Puffin.
Doherty, Berlie (1995) *Children of Winter*. Mammoth.
Downing, David (2001) *J. F. Kennedy* (Leading Lives series). Heinemann Library.
Dutton, Richard (ed.) (1996) *Midsummer Night's Dream by William Shakespeare*. Macmillan.
Filipovic, Zlata (1995) *Zlata's Diary*. Puffin.
Fischel, Emma (1998) *William Shakespeare* (Famous People, Famous Lives series). Franklin Watts.
Geras, Adele (1996) *Beauty and the Beast and Other Stories*, retold by Adele Geras. Hamilton.
Haddon, Mark (1990s series) *Agent Z Stories*. Red Fox.
Hughes, Ted (1994) *The Iron Man*. Faber.
Impey, Rose (1990s series) *Creepies*. Collins.
Kliman, Bernice W. (1995) *Macbeth* (Shakespeare in Performance series). Manchester University Press.
Lee, Carol Ann (2001) *Anne Frank's Story*. Puffin.
Morpurgo, Michael (1998) *Arthur, High King of Britain*. Pavilion.
Naidoo, Beverley (1985) *Journey to Jo'burg*. Longman.
Pratt, Richard (2001) *Pirate Diary: The Journal of Jake Carpenter*. Walker.
Ridley, Philip (1994) *Kaspar and the Glitter*. Viking.
Scieszka, Jon and Smith, Lane (1993) *The Stinky Cheeseman and Other Fairly Stupid Tales*. Puffin.
Sendak, Maurice (1967) *Where the Wild Things Are*. Bodley Head.
Sewell, Anna (1999) *Black Beauty*. Penguin.
Steptoe, John (1997) *Mufaro's Beautiful Daughters*. Puffin.
Sutcliff, Rosemary (1995) *Wanderings of Odysseus*. Frances Lincoln.
Tolkien, J. R. R. (1998) *The Hobbit*. Collins.
Turnbull, Ann (1996) *Friends and Foes*. Walker.
Ure, Jean (1989) *A Tea-leaf on the Roof*. Magnet/Methuen.
Vivelo, Jackie (1994) *Chills Run Down My Spine*. Dorling Kindersley.
Waddell, Martin (1994) *Owl Babies*. Walker.

Reference

Doonan, Jane (1993) *Looking at Pictures in Picture Books*. Thimble Press.
Opie, Iona and Opie, Peter (1959) *The Lore and Language of Schoolchildren*. Clarendon Press.